PARADISE LOST

PARADISE LOST

The Struggle for Celtic's Soul

Michael Kelly

Best wishes,

Mick Kelly

CANONGATE PRESS

First published in Great Britain in 1994 by
Canongate Press Ltd.
14 Frederick Street
Edinburgh EH2 2HB

ISBN 0 86241 506 3

British Library Cataloguing-in-Publication Data

A catalogue record for this book is available on request
from the British Library

Typeset by Hewer Text Composition Services, Edinburgh
Printed and bound in Great Britain by
Redwood Books, Trowbridge

*For real Celtic supporters
everywhere —
in case their children ask.*

Author's Acknowledgements

Thanks to Mike Stanger, who had the idea for this book three years ago, and whose help made sure I finished it.

Zita gave me unstinting support during four years that were harder on her than on me. So did the kids. And Maureen.

It is not appropriate to thank Chris and David. We were all in this together. But I was proud to work with them as we tried to safeguard the traditions that we all believed in. And proud to leave with them.

Thanks to Vincent, for helping me keep a sense of perspective.

. . . Such as for their bellies' sake,
Creep and climb into the fold.
Of other care they little reckoning make,
Than how to scramble at the shearers' feast,

And shove away the worthy bidden guest.
Blind mouths! that scarce themselves know how to hold
A sheep-hook, or have learn'd aught else the least
That to the faithful herdsman's art belongs!

John Milton, *Lycidas*, 1637

Introduction

PARADISE LOST

Conceived in vengeance, born in deceit – that was the campaign conducted against the Board of Celtic Football Club from 1990 to 1994.

The roots of the struggles go back to the decline of the Club on and off the field in the late 1970s and the 1980s – a decade and more before I joined the Board. Football had changed and the pace of change was increasing, but Celtic did not match the momentum and was falling behind. The failure of the Board at that time to take the steps necessary to introduce professional management to deal with the problems and meet the challenges left the Club vulnerable to approaches from outside. And there were many approaches – from more or less scrupulous people who wanted to 'help' Celtic by injecting their cash, their expertise and, always, by assuming control.

Two more such people soon appeared on the horizon. In 1988 Fergus McCann, an expatriate Scot living in French Canada, who had made his money marketing Scottish golfing holidays, offered to re-finance the Club in exchange for 51% of the shares. The Board declined his help, but rather in 1990 co-opted Brian Dempsey, a property developer believed by many to be the kind of businessman Celtic needed. I was also invited to join at the same time, with my public relations and ex-Lord Provost's credentials.

Dempsey's subsequent removal by me and Chris White, the Club secretary, generated in him a humiliation which lasted three and a half years. He sought to expunge this blow to his self-esteem by campaigning against us and everything we then did to effect necessary and beneficial change to Celtic.

In 1991, Dempsey hired David St. Clair Low, a 'financial adviser' whose ego I had apparently failed to stroke sufficiently, to organise an assault against Celtic which did grave damage to the Club, the team and its supporters. When news of this 'carefully-planned campaign' broke in the Press, Low denied it. On the first page of his recent account of the campaign that succeeded in bringing the Club to its knees as a means to gaining control (*Rebels in Paradise*, David Low and Francis Shennan, Edinburgh 1994), Low admits brazenly to this – and later to persuading Kevin McCarra of *Scotland on Sunday* that the rumours about a consortium formed to take over the Club 'were unfounded'.

When such a person offers the humiliated a chance for redress, then you can be certain that money will change hands. Low was paid money for his part in the venture. Exactly how much his inside story fails to reveal, although he received a cheque from the rebels for over £16,000 in February 1994. For what services over what period is not clear – maybe some journalist will ask him some day.

One of the first things Low did was to buy a copy of *The Prince*, to ensure that every Machiavellian ploy was used. One tactic appears to have been to portray me as the devious character, an idea which found its way into *Scotland on Sunday* when it ran a profile of me. No wonder the struggle for Celtic's soul was lost.

If someone boasts of using Machiavellian tactics – which the Shorter Oxford English Dictionary defines as 'preferring expediency to morality' and 'practising duplicity' – is it not fair to ask exactly what this involved? Obviously, lying. What else was done? Bribing journalists? Bribing anyone else? Blackmailing anyone? Threatening anyone? Whatever the answers, his admissions prove that we were right not to trust him with any role in Celtic's future.

The three of us, David Smith, Chris White and I, who resigned rather than work with these people, did none of these things. We were concerned to do what was best for Celtic. We were trying to achieve a long-term solution to the Club's problems. And we were selective about the methods we used. The end never justifies questionable means, especially so when an institution founded on principles of justice and charity is involved. We saw the depths to which the other side would stoop. But it never entered our heads to follow. This was not naïvety. We had our rules and we obeyed them. It was a case of mythical kings versus iguanas.

Chris even refused to allow me to begin the buying of the

shares of smaller shareholders, because it was against the tradition of the Club for the shares to have anything more than a deep emotional value. He was not going to be party to their reduction to the status of mere financial instruments.

We also eschewed any campaign of denigrating our opponents in the Press. For years the Press and public were puzzled as to why we removed Dempsey from the Board. I don't know what he told them. But one of the reasons our story was not told was that if I had tried to explain it I would have been accused of starting a dirty tricks campaign. I didn't want Celtic associated with anything like that. The pathetic attempt of our opponents in 1992 to dub the proposed spoof in the Club's newspaper, the *Celtic View*, a 'smear plot' demonstrates the lengths to which they went to try to discredit us – and how little evidence they had.

Naturally, we wanted to stay in charge. But we always had our eyes on what was best for Celtic, combining our duties to the shareholders with our deep-felt desire to restore its football fortunes. The rebels wanted control without regard to the effect on either, so that every proposal and initiative we made was attacked irrespective of its merits.

And the Scottish Press went along with them. Its treatment of the Celtic story is an object lesson in all that is wrong with the media, and a solid argument for reform, restrictions and redress. The reporting was one-sided and the Press was partial. For the rest of the season after the takeover, Celtic's results were worse and the gates were lower than any under the old Board. Yet this was glossed over or ignored, whereas with us it was manufactured into crisis headlines.

Running a PR business means talking daily to journalists. I started off as a director with good personal relationships with them and their editors. They also knew my track record, which was excellent. Yet, for the sake of stories which they must have known were inaccurate (the rebels' books list the lies they told), they ignored that relationship and track record. They refused to translate the credibility I had with them into balanced judgement. It may seem to them that this criticism is personal, but that is true only in one or two isolated instances. What I am condemning is the transformation of the concept of a free Press into a commercial machine where truth, accuracy and balance are sacrificed for sensation, circulation and profit.

The most depressing aspect of the whole affair was the behaviour of that part of the Celtic support which allowed itself to be organised against us. These people sent me death threats and excrement through the post. They shouted abuse at my wife as we walked into Celtic Park. They accosted my daughter in a disco. Yet there was no Press campaign against this – these people buy papers, you know. And Dominic Keane, financial expert, director of fourteen companies and now company secretary of Celtic, was caught by BBC TV shaking his fist and seemingly encouraging hooligans as they chanted their intolerant abuse in front of the stadium.

Even more dangerous and juvenile is Low's sentimental identification of himself and his colleagues with the rebels in Northern Ireland. Low describes Cushendall as a 'safe haven' because 'it had a tendency to sympathise with rebels being a nationalist area'. Pandering to the ignorant feelings and romantic attachments of louts living safe from the tragic realities of violence is nauseating and against all the traditions of Celtic.

Low claims that in his work with Bremners plc 'his job was to get a good deal for shareholders'. This is a paramount duty of directors, but in the case of Celtic, the rebels were not prepared to recognise that this was our duty too. Their surrogates on the Board turned down an offer of £300 per share in preference to a much less favourable deal. But that deal was one which, more importantly for them, saved their skins – or so they thought.

The struggle for Celtic's soul was lost, in the last analysis, because Kevin, my cousin and the Club chairman, did a deal behind our backs with the people we had opposed for three years . . . people who despised and ridiculed him. He sold Celtic short because he was unable to comprehend the situation that we were in, the real choice that he had on 3 March 1994 and was confused by the rebels' lies and blandishments. We were at fault in not holding Kevin's hand in that last week. But by then David was fed up to the teeth wet-nursing him. If Kevin argues that he abandoned us because he was kept in the dark, then it is only an excuse.

Tom Grant, another director, sold us out too. Perhaps I was stupid to expect more from him, despite the fact that he had voluntarily entered into the shareholders' agreement with us for mutual support. He had changed sides so many times that it was obvious that he was interested only in his own survival.

But Kevin should not have acted as he did. A week after I had agreed to resign, I asked him why he had kept secret from me the fateful meeting with the bank on 3 March. 'Because you would have been against what we were going to do' was the answer that confirmed the clandestine nature of the affair.

Quite simply, we made the mistake of trusting Kevin – at least to the extent of expecting him to tell us that he disagreed with our policy and wanted to pursue another route. Instead he told me, after a Board meeting carefully planned but called at ten minutes' notice so that we could not attend, that David and Chris had been suspended from all executive duties.

We also made a mistake, as we swiftly prepared for the news conference on 26 February 1994, in not having Superstadia's construction guarantors, Gefinor, sufficiently-well briefed to withstand the hostile publicity which the announcement of the funding package for Cambuslang received. We should not have disclosed their name before being sure that they would not wilt under fire. But then, of course, the announcement would have been given even less credibility.

We also underestimated the determination of the Bank of Scotland to unload the Celtic debt. The bank knew that it was David and nobody else who was managing the Club, and that David, in his other business dealings, had made and saved the bank considerable sums of money. Given the long-term relationship of over one hundred years that the Club had with the bank, we were justified in expecting that the bank would not sell him out. But it did.

How far McCann was aware of the underhand methods used to undermine Celtic is not clear. In fairness to him, from the very first approach that he made to the Club his proposals and demands remained consistent. He would put capital in, but he wanted control. But he was extremely difficult to deal with. His proposals hardly varied from 1989, from which time he knew that handing over control was an unacceptable condition. Instead of using the frequent discussions with directors – before and after I joined the Board – to find an acceptable solution which combined his injection of capital with the retention of the family tradition, he simply reiterated his demands. A more flexible, less obdurate person would have recognised the stumbling block and attempted to remove it amicably. With better faith he could have been a substantial participant in the solution that we proposed on 26 February 1994.

I found him difficult to understand, never more so than in June 1993, when he faxed me an offer in a simple, almost naïve, way. It called for acceptance by return of a proposition removing us from control. It was clearly unreasonable to expect an immediate answer to the issue at the heart of the problem. Did McCann seriously expect an immediate acceptance, or was he setting us up? I still don't know. But even two months after the takeover, he claimed that my replies were an attempt to stonewall him, whereas what I had proposed was an immediate meeting.

David and I had met him in Montreal the previous June, when we exhorted him not to throw in his lot with a group who were simply interested in seizing control from us. He apparently resisted doing so for some time. One of the reasons that they turned to him was that they did not have enough money themselves – something which he discovered when he asked them to match their promises with actions. As he has succeeded in his goal, he will no doubt feel that his eventual decision to go with the rebels was justified. It may be, however, that the tactics which they used, which finally resulted in his successful takeover, have destroyed the very values that made him a Celtic supporter in the first place.

Because I am in no doubt that the Celtic ethic is dead. The Club will continue as a football team. It will, hopefully, have renewed success. But it is now just another football team. The moral authority whereby it could claim to represent a culture and fulfill a broader community role has been removed.

That was the heritage that we were guarding. That was the role we tried to fulfil, and at which others sneered. That was the reason we wanted to safeguard the Club by relocating and refinancing it at Cambuslang in a way which Dempsey himself had favoured at Robroyston. Despite everything, I believe we did our duty by our forefathers, for the Club and for its supporters.

The saddest thing is that those who participated in the act of vandalism that has destroyed Celtic do not yet realise what they have done.

Of the two other books purporting to be the inside story of the sell-out of Celtic, Allan Caldwell's *Sack the Board!* (Edinburgh,

1994) has to be dismissed. It is not a serious attempt to describe or explain what happened. Caldwell was the freelance journalist who supplied most of the anti-Board stories to the *Evening Times*. He was close to Dempsey and Dempsey has written the foreword to his book. That tells the tale.

Caldwell indulges, badly, in the factional school of historical analysis. He gets most of the trivia, which he inserts to lighten the text, wrong. Thus he furnishes my house with lace curtains, which we have never had, clothes me in a dressing gown I don't own, and has McCann playing an eight iron in Arizona as his telephone rang at home. How could he possibly know? This is not history. This is word-painting. But he gets the colours wrong, so wrong that the picture itself is unrecognisable.

Low's *Rebels in Paradise* demands more attention. He worked his way inside the rebel camp after he saw no future for himself with the Board. He became an adviser to Dempsey, earning good money for his concern for Celtic. His book confirms my view that we were working against an unscrupulous campaign. His espousal of Machiavelli, on the basis of that political thinker's poorest work, is immature but significant. From the very first page of his book, Low not only admits to lying, but is proud to acknowledge it as part of his armoury. Thus on pages 9, 16, 17, 23, 70, 81, 91, 98 and 99 we get references to deceptions, of one form or another, that were perpetrated to advance their cause.

I stopped counting after page 99, because that contained what should be a most embarrassing admission from someone who likes to describe himself as a 'financial expert', someone who has been 'head of investment' at a stockbrokers, and 'chairman of a public company'. Jimmy Farrell, yet another director, and Low were looking at Celtic documents that Farrell was legally entitled to see. He had appointed Low as his 'assistant'. Low tells us that there were certain papers that he should not have been looking at, but that 'he looked at as many documents as he could, entitled to or not. He had been reminding his fellow rebels for weeks that they were playing to win. This was food and drink to him. He was practising what he preached.' He contrasts his duplicity with our approach when he records, with surprise, that a phone call to the bank confirmed that 'Smith had been telling the truth'. He always did.

Low was not a real Celtic person. But that was the hallmark of the rebels' campaign.

Chapter One

Nor war, nor battle's sound
Was heard the world around,
The idle spear and shield were high up hung...

John Milton, *On the Morning of Christ's Nativity* (1629), 1.53

The Sixties really did swing for Celtic fans. We won the Cup in 1965 and the next year began our march toward the world record of nine League wins in a row. And Lisbon – that was the ultimate! Celtic, the first British club to win the European Cup, and with an entire team of Scots.

Every Celtic fan can remember where he or she was on that famous Ascension Thursday night. Most now claim to have been in the National Stadium, which would have had to expand its capacity to 200,000 to accommodate all the claimants. Me? I was at home watching the game on TV. I had a flying phobia which not even the prospect of a European Final could help me overcome. I had also just started a new job at the University of Strathclyde on 1 April 1965, so the extra days needed for an overland trip were simply not available in the busy third term.

So, with my mother, father and sister, I watched the match in black and white. Earlier in the day, I had attended Mass on this Holiday of Obligation at the city centre church of St Aloysius. The Jesuit celebrating the Mass called for prayers for Celtic.

As the teams ran on to the field I felt we needed all the help that we could get. This was Inter Milan that we were playing. The cunning successors to Machiavelli, they were the masters of *catenacio*. We had only a bunch of guys from Glasgow, whose flyest trick was to miss training with a 'cold'. When Inter went one-up with a penalty needlessly given away by Craig, it confirmed our worst fears about the size of the task. But prayer, and the collective will of three generations of down-trodden Irish immigrants in heaven and on the terracing, with a little assistance from Stein's tactical genius, were equal to it and produced an incredible equaliser and a sensational winner.

The objectives of those who established Celtic in the poor East End of Glasgow had been achieved. The discriminated had equalled the best. The outcasts had been accepted. The oppressed could hold their heads high. The dissenters were part of the establishment. Many other organisations, having been so successful in achieving their goals, would have been wound up. You can't do that with a football club – but possibly a lack of clear purpose from then on contributed to the period of drift the Club eventually entered in the mid-Seventies.

As a boy I had been weaned on stories of Celtic's successes in the Twenties and Thirties. But those who had told those stories were forced to admit that nothing achieved back then had remotely approached the Stein years. Jock Stein gave Celtic the team of the fans' dreams. It was he who proved correct the musings of old men to their children, because an examination of Celtic's inter-war record shows a respectable performance but not an outstanding one. In the myths, however, the players of these years were giants and their achievements legendary. We all believed them – maybe Stein did too, for how else could he dare think of scaling the heights that he did? Whatever the reason, he justified retrospectively our delusions of grandeur.

'Celtic was my life' sounds like the worst kind of maudlin exaggeration. But I cannot think of anything which has given me such emotional highs and lows. The Bill Shankly aphorism that football is more important than life and death is clearly rubbish. A night at a sick child's bedside quickly restores your sense of values. Health, family and friends are always going to rank higher. But thousands of Celtic supporters will identify with the utter dependence on the Saturday result to the enjoyment of the weekend. They know the thrill of anticipation from early on a Saturday morning. They know the despair of losing a goal, the joy of the equaliser, the ecstasy of the winner and the triumph of the final whistle. Especially at Ibrox. And there is no better feeling than waking up on a Sunday morning with the realisation that you have won the Cup.

There is also the extraordinary confidence that Celtic supporters have. In 1986, to win the League we had to go to Love Street, beat St. Mirren at least three-nothing and have Hearts lose to Dundee. I knew we would do it. The same belief emanated from the support as we rolled up. It is through such telepathy that the binding together of a support occurs. I got involved in that result. BBC TV gave the half-time score from Dens Park as one-nothing for Dundee. As I walked out of the tea room, Bobby Lennox came up from the dug-out looking for information. Rumours are notorious at football matches, but I had seen this with my own eyes so I told him. As he went down to relay the information to Davie Hay, the BBC corrected the score to nothing each. I agonised over trying to get a message to the dug-out in case the false information would change the tactics. I needn't have worried. Football management isn't that sophisticated.

I went to my first game in 1947 and remember sitting quietly in Row C of the old Directors' Box, and as it got darker being fascinated by lights which appeared magically to flash around the terracing opposite. It was much later that I realised they were the sparks of dozens of cigarette lighters.

Celtic was the dominant topic of conversation at home. My father was proud of his father's role in the formation of the Club and repeatedly told me his version of history. At this time Celtic was going through one of its worst spells and there was great discontent over the performance of the manager, Jimmy McGrory, who had been appointed by my uncle, Bob Kelly. My father claimed that he and Desmond White, another director, had approached Matt Busby, who was willing to come as manager. They planned to move his appointment at the next AGM. Bob got wind of the idea, took it as a challenge to his power and secured enough proxy votes to block the move. This started a family feud between my father and his brother, which was never resolved even during Bob Kelly's long terminal illness in 1970.

The whole thing was incredibly petty. My father and mother didn't let it stop them going to games – indeed they always went to the Directors' Box, and took me and my sister with them. But Bob and my father ignored each other and my father would not go into the Board Room for hospitality. So we stood outside in the entrance hall under the John Thomson Memorial, waiting until it was time to go up to our seats. Every Saturday for years Bob would walk past us and ignore my father. And, of course, this coldness was extended (by association) to me. It baffled me.

10

Naturally, all this drama made me even more interested in the Celtic stories, and my father never tired of repeating them. He made me conscious that the Kelly family went back to the very foundation of the Club through my grandfather, James Kelly. He was the son of an Irish immigrant, David Kelly, who was recorded in the 1840 census as being a hammerman in Alexandria. James Kelly played football for Renton in the 1880s when they were champions of the world. As the best known Catholic player of the time, it was natural that, when the Irish community in Glasgow decided to found a football team, they turned to him to be its first signing and captain. He later became a substantial shareholder and chairman, remaining as a director until his death in 1931 when his son Bob took his place.

But I had a double family connection. In that original Celtic team, playing alongside Jimmy Kelly, was Michael Dunbar, my mother's uncle and the person after whom I was named. He served as a director of the Club from 1897 to 1921. So my mother was as well-versed in Celtic affairs as my father, and as keen a supporter. There was no sexism in the Kelly household, even at a time when football was very much a male preserve.

Our house was littered with football memorabilia – winners' medals, Scottish caps, photographs – which we kids would take out every so often to pore over. And to hear the same stories repeated, again and again. The themes were always the same: how proud we should be of the family connection; how the Club restored pride to an oppressed immigrant community; how religious tolerance had come to hallmark Celtic; how important Celtic was to thousands of people. And this was all emphasised in the passionate discussion we heard among the constant stream of visiting friends and relatives.

It is easy to see how this environment tailored my thinking about Celtic and set in my mind the values that must be upheld and the traditions that must be safeguarded.

The frustration and agony of my childhood was that Celtic's performance on the field was abysmal. So the stories seemed like dreams. Eventually, by the late Fifties, I don't know whether I still believed them or not.

There was the occasional highlight. I remember, as everybody of my age claims to, Danny Kaye appearing on the field at Hampden before an Old Firm Charity Cup Final which Celtic won. My first glimpse of Rangers in action was awesome. They seemed to fill their solid blue shirts with bodies much bulkier than the Celts, who seemed to be made smaller by their hoops. Rangers' black socks added a touch of menace. And when my Aunt Bride, sitting beside me, told me that the right back who had just brought down Charlie Tully was called 'Tiger' Shaw, the picture that I still have of Rangers as the enemy was complete.

This belief that Rangers recruited big physical players had some basis in fact. Willie Waddell once dismissed Jimmy Johnstone as 'a wee ball player', expressing a preference for 'strong direct forwards'. But I suspect the idea had more to do with the persistent defeats they inflicted on Celtic throughout the Forties and Fifties. Certainly, the illusion was ruined by the arrival of designer football shirts. Rangers never posed the same threat in dressy clothes. But, of course, that was after Stein had reduced the giants to pigmies.

There were also two Cup Final victories in the Fifties. John McPhail beat Motherwell with the only goal of the game and Sean Fallon amazed everyone — including himself, I suspect — by scoring one of the two goals that beat Aberdeen. There was no room for me in the Directors' Box at Hampden and I was relegated to the Press Box, much to the irritation of one scribe who arrived too late for a seat. Sports journalists are still as charming. I was put beside Peter Thomson who was commentating for BBC radio. He greeted me with: 'I hope you don't swear.' I was twelve and I simply didn't know how to take this, so it shut me up for the whole game. I now realise he was trying to be funny. But he wasn't a very good commentator either.

Celtic did win the Coronation Cup against Scottish and English competition in 1953. But the highlight of the Fifties was the seven-one victory over Rangers in the 1957 League Cup Final. I was at boarding school and was playing rugby for the first fifteen against Hillhead High School that afternoon. On my return to the dormitory I was greeted with the unbelievable news. Certainly that result helped sustain the ardour of Celtic fans throughout a very barren period because that was the last trophy the team won until the Stein era. It was also unusual in that Celtic got a penalty. Given the well-established preference of the referees of that era (and any other, come to think of it),

12

this was a major upset. It led Celtic fans to joke that any time we were six-one up against Rangers the referee would give us a penalty.

These were very brief highlights indeed at a time when Rangers were having huge successes. Celtic struggled to the occasional Cup Final. But a combination of bad management and eccentric team selection by Bob Kelly ensured defeat. First, in 1955, Clyde won a replay after Bob dropped Bobby Collins. Then, in my one and only Celtic game on the Hampden terracing, Hearts won the Cup when Bob ignored regular first team players to field Billy Craig in one of his first games and moved right back Mike Haughney up to the forward line.

Two other Finals were lost, partly through mysterious team selections. First, the 1961 Cup Final, when we were beaten two-nothing by Dunfermline after a replay (although that was a defeat future events would demand, as Stein was the Dunfermline manager). And, after another Cup Final defeat by Rangers in the 1963 replay, it wasn't until 1965 that I saw Celtic win the Cup again. Indeed, Bertie Auld's goal when he headed the rebound from Charlie Gallagher's shot into the net was the first time I had ever seen Celtic equalise in a final! Years later, Stein confirmed to me that goal and that win were the most significant ones of his career as Celtic manager. 'That made the rest possible,' he said.

That was during one of the few conversations I had with him, trying to establish if he knew what had made him so successful. He couldn't explain it. I fed him suggestions about psychology, planning, homework. But he was unable to articulate what was clearly an innate talent. He kept saying, 'It was the players.' But we knew it wasn't. We had seen them before he arrived.

It seems incredible now, but Bob Kelly got away with this gross interference in what was clearly the manager's province. His amateurish approach to team matters and strangely irrational selection decisions virtually guaranteed Celtic's failure to win anything from 1957 to 1963. He acquired a tremendous reputation as a football administrator, for which work he was eventually knighted. But as a manager he was a disaster. This was a topic that dominated family conferences. But no one could move Bob. He was not the eldest son, but he was probably the sharpest. When his father died, he moved to replace him on the various companies of which he was a director, including Celtic.

13

Bob Kelly was a difficult, stubborn man. But he was a man of principle, integrity and strong moral conviction. One of the moments I felt proudest of him was when Celtic protested against the inclusion in the European Cup of countries from Eastern Europe after the Russian invasion of Czechoslovakia in 1968 – that followed Celtic's tradition. The Club also refused numerous invitations from Southern Africa during the years of white-minority, racist rule – a fact I delighted in telling Nelson Mandela personally on his visit to Glasgow in 1993 as I handed him his Celtic scarf.

Bob was also deeply religious. Indeed, there was a suspicion in the early Sixties that he was trying to create an all-Catholic team. To some, credence was given to this by his dropping of Bertie Peacock for the 1961 Cup Final replay against Dunfermline, and his transfer of Bertie Auld. But the fact that it was he who appointed Stein as manager, the first Protestant to hold the job, gives the lie to that.

That news was broken by the *Sunday Express* on the last Sunday in January 1965. It was the best thing that ever happened to me as a Celtic supporter. I phoned the *Express* office in Glasgow for confirmation on the Sunday, because no one could believe that Bob would hand over power the way that an autocrat like Stein would demand. But he did, Stein's only concession being to agree to Sean Fallon's being his assistant.

There is a marvellous story told of Stein's first day at Celtic Park. He was replacing Jimmy McGrory, who had been Stein's manager and who was being kept on as press officer. Relations between the two were bound to be awkward to start with. But Stein showed his brilliance as a man-manager by striding into the crowded dressing room and walking straight up to McGrory with the words, 'How are you, Boss?'

I had seen the same psychology in action a year earlier when Stein, then manager of Dunfermline, came back to watch a reserve game. He was standing at the dressing room door as the Celtic team came out and saw Jimmy Johnstone, who had been dropped from the first team. 'What are you doing playing with this lot?' Stein shouted out in his Lanarkshire miner's voice. 'You're far too good for the reserves.' Johnstone scored a hat-trick.

I was twenty-three when Stein arrived, and my indoctrination in Celtic principles had been completed. I accepted that there was as much pain as pleasure in being a football supporter – and, if your team was Celtic, maybe more. But, of course, supporting a team is not a matter of choice. You're stuck with it, just like you're stuck with your nationality. And the fact that the feats of the Twenties and Thirties had never been remotely approached since was a cause of frustration and depression, not a reason for seeking another team.

It was clear, anyway, that Celtic was as much of a way of life as a football team. The values were clear and they were repeated by the countless visitors to our home who always wanted to discuss the team. I heard them at school and at university. All young Celtic supporters had inherited the same philosophy: Celtic represented the Irish Catholic in Scotland. Celtic stood for the underdog. Celtic was anti-establishment. Celtic represented social justice and opposed discrimination.

And the role of the Kellys in ensuring these values were retained was central. I was reminded of this again and again. A Kelly had been the first player, a Kelly had been an early chairman, a Kelly was the current chairman. And another Kelly would succeed him.

I was also told how a Kelly at Celtic Park should behave. There was always to be a distance from the players. Support should be enthusiastic but not boisterous. The other team and its supporters were to be respected. And the game and any enmity finished at twenty-to-five.

That was the Celtic way.

Chapter Two

What though the field be lost?
All is not lost; th' unconquerable will . . .

John Milton, *Paradise Lost*, 1.105

My first meeting with Fergus McCann was just as unconventional as all the others.

One summer afternoon in 1989, I got a phone call from a partner in Maclay, Murray and Spens – one of Scotland's leading firms of solicitors – asking if I would meet Fergus McCann, 'who wants to take over Celtic'. I was fairly well-used to people wanting to bite my ear about Celtic, even though I was not at that time a director. But the directness of this approach amused me. So I cleared my diary to see him in my city centre office.

McCann does not make a good first impression – small, bespectacled and balding. He appears eccentric. This impression was reinforced every time I met him. In a television age, appearance is vital and his may yet prove a severe disadvantage if things are not going well at Celtic Park. But he came straight to the point. He told me of the correspondence, meetings and discussions he had recently had with the Celtic directors. He told me that his offers of a large financial injection had been rebuffed in what he considered a rude and unbusinesslike way. He told me that he wanted 51% of the shares: this didn't seem to him a good enough reason for his plan to be rejected.

His view was simple. Celtic was going nowhere. It needed capital and professional management. He was rich and he could point to a successful track record in marketing. The Board and the shareholders should hand him control for five years and let him get on with it.

His analysis of the situation echoed much of what I thought myself – particularly with regard to the lack of inspiration or leadership shown by the chairman, Jack McGinn.

But I just could not take Fergus seriously. I could see that he was quirky and prickly and I was amazed at his apparent ignorance of my position viz-a-viz the directors. I thought he wanted to recruit me as a family shareholder to intercede on his behalf. But he didn't seem to know where I fitted in to the Celtic set-up. He had accepted his solicitor's suggestion that he needed PR advice and had come to me on their recommendation.

He insisted on outlining the proposal which he had put in writing to McGinn on 30 June 1989, and supplied me with a written copy. Referring to a meeting with McGinn on 4 January 1989 and a reply from Celtic on 28 April 1989, he registered his disappointment that his offer had been thrown out, especially as Chris had not put forward an alternative. He then outlined how he thought that his 'abilities and funds could effectively be applied for the good of the Club' while meeting Celtic's objections. He concluded that the best solution was that the needs of all the different parties could only be met 'through direct equity investment with various special provisions'.

The letter was primarily to give the Board advanced warning that he intended shortly (12 July!) to make an offer to purchase at least 51% of the Celtic shares. He was going to offer £110 for each £1 issued share, £50 in cash and £60 in new 8% Celtic Cumulative Preference Shares. This would amount to £2.2 million.

On top of that, McCann would invest additional capital of £3.0 million. At the same time he would provide cash or securities as collateral for bank borrowing of £2.2 million. The total of money in the deal was therefore £7.4 million.

He promised to forego any interest or dividends on his money for five years and would give the new preferred shareholders a right of veto on the sale of his shares for five years and a right of first refusal if he wanted to sell. He was prepared to allow the present directors to stay on the Board, and if they were executives, in their jobs. He offered a meeting to discuss details, to 'respond to any concerns' and to 'discuss possible modifications to this package'. But he urged the directors to recommend it to shareholders. He saw his proposal as the way to 'relieve the pressure to operate with a lack of capital and costly bank financing secured over the Club's assets'.

As for the shareholders, 'while receiving a substantial cash payment will continue to have an important, income-producing stake in Celtic and the knowledge that its control remains in friendly hands'.

And the supporters 'will have the assurance that the Club is properly capitalised, able to provide a Park to be proud of ... and has a secure financial base to maintain and improve its competitive position on the field'.

On the basis of the discussions he had already had with Chris and McGinn, Fergus anticipated rejection of his offer. He planned to go over the heads of the directors and shareholders to the public. He wanted me to handle the PR campaign.

I pointed out my close connection with the Board, and told him I could not possibly work on his behalf. I imagine my poor relationship with McCann stemmed from that moment. Instead, I directed him to Barkers. They have acted for him ever since – and I would guess they have commanded fees four times anything that my company received from Celtic in later years. Again, despite all the 'inside stories', those fees he incurred have not been revealed, but cheques for nearly £20,000 were paid.

The offer must have seemed to Fergus a reasonable one, pumping £7.4 million into a small private company. If Celtic had been an ordinary commercial concern, the shareholders would have bitten his hand off in their rush to grab the largesse! But my view was that the offer was destined to be rejected, because it was based on a complete misunderstanding of the aspirations of the directors and shareholders.

This informal offer document talked about giving shareholders 'a substantial cash payment'. But Celtic shareholders had never regarded their shares as having any monetary value at all. The share certificates were pieces of paper to be handed down from generation to generation, with strict instructions that they were not to be sold.

It promised that directors would 'maintain their present positions' and 'much of their power', whereas Fergus's 51% in fact would guarantee *him* control. There was therefore no chance whatsoever of the directors (of whom I was not yet one) agreeing to sit back and watch Fergus run the Club. His eccentric appearance and behaviour completely put them off. More importantly, no one was convinced that his North American marketing experience would translate readily into the unsophisticated bazaar of Scottish football.

Deducting what was to be paid to shareholders, Fergus's offer would have in effect injected £5 million pounds into the Club. While that might just have been enough to transform it, Fergus was not, in my outsider's view, offering a realistic price to the owners for the transfer of control. He was proposing to pay the equivalent of £100 a share. He was proposing to acquire half of Celtic for a million pounds. He was proposing to take control for the price of a player.

No Celtic shareholder would have accepted that. And they would have been right because, three years later, in 1992, shares were changing hands at £350 per share. In the case of any 'normal' business, an increase in the price of shares would be regarded as a sure sign of a valued asset. I have often wondered why people didn't recognise that the spectacular increase in share price vindicated the directors' refusal to accept lower offers.

Nevertheless, it is hard to see what offer Fergus could have made in 1989 that would have been acceptable to the then Board and the shareholders. He wanted control and the shareholders were not prepared to give it up. He wanted to run the Club and the directors were not going to move over for him. From my seat on the sidelines, it seemed certain his bid would fail.

McCann was just one of many people who 'wanted to help the Club'. Virtually every Celtic supporter who could in any way describe himself as a businessman came forward with a proposal to supply capital or management expertise or both.

The reason was obvious. Celtic lacked leadership and direction. The Club had been drifting for many years, but it may be convenient to date the decline from the death of Desmond White in 1984. Neither Bob Kelly nor Desmond could be regarded as ideal leaders. They were too close to being dictators for that. But with their tyranny they at least brought certainty and decision. No one was in any doubt as to where control lay, or who you had to convince if you wanted something approved.

But both had the fault shared by all despots – neither of them made proper plans for the succession. Bob Kelly suffered a long and painful illness before his death, which he bore with great fortitude and resignation. But, although he resigned from the Board to become president and to allow Desmond White to take over the chair, he never sought to replace himself – not even with his nephew, Kevin, who did not join the Board until after Bob's death.

Desmond, hearty and fit to the end, was one of those people

who did not expect to die. So that, when he took a fatal heart attack on a scuba diving holiday in Greece, no contingency plans had been prepared.

The job of chairman went to Tom Devlin on the basis of 'Buggin's Turn'. Tom was a cheery old bloke – with no discernible talent whatsoever. He had owned a trawler fleet in Leith which he sold in the 1950s and had been retired ever since. A hypochondriac, he took genuinely and seriously ill shortly after becoming chairman and died in office. During his period of office, he did nothing at all. His considerable shareholding went to his widow, Betty, whose understanding of the emerging football business was even more slender than her husband's.

After Tom Devlin's death, the inevitable scramble occurred for the chairmanship – between McGinn and Farrell. So naked was their ambition that no discussion of a possible outside candidate was allowed at Board level. The opportunity to inject some modern management thinking into the Club was lost.

Farrell was the more senior in terms of service. He fully expected the job. McGinn, however, lobbied Chris White very hard. Chris recognised that his father had co-opted himself and McGinn onto the Board on the same day, having exacted a promise from McGinn that he would 'look after Chris' when Desmond was unable to do so. The largest shareholder as a result of his inheritance from his father, Chris plumped for McGinn to be chairman.

McGinn liked to allude to his background in newspapers, which may have given the impression that he was some kind of journalist. In fact, he worked on the distribution side, calling on newsagents to check that they were getting the correct numbers of *Daily Expresses*. Such a skill, though a vital cog in any media empire, was not precisely the kind of experience that Celtic needed in the late 1980s.

Like all such persons who find themselves in positions of apparent prestige and power, McGinn seemed to believe his talents were real. It is a phenomenon that I first observed among local government councillors. I detected the same syndrome among a number of football directors who served on the SFA or Scottish League committees. McGinn epitomised both.

This self-deceptive illness is brought on by the excessive attention of competent officials, who do all the detailed work on complex issues but who prudently encourage their elected bosses to take the credit. Most of these 'bosses' are happy to believe they have themselves solved the problems. They actually delude themselves that they are rather smart individuals. They then begin to behave in the way they think successful people carry on.

I have observed many times at first hand that this behaviour includes a self-conscious way of walking into a room or a patronising manner of discoursing on subjects those afflicted know nothing whatsover about. It also leads to frequent bouts of foreign travel where the individuals 'learn lessons that they can apply at home'.

Anyway, it was this kind of person – the sort who struggles with past participles and who has difficulty with the pronunciation of 'lunAtic' – who was now chairman of the Celtic Football and Athletic Company Ltd. For a Club founded by a member of a Catholic teaching order, it was hard to reconcile.

So it is little wonder that the fans saw the Club going nowhere fast. An extension to the main stand for the centenary celebrations in 1988 added on much-needed hospitality facilities. While they were of themselves of a highly acceptable standard, the development was a piecemeal one and not part of any coherent overall long-term plan. In particular, the cost of the development drove the overdraft up.

At the same time, Rangers were making unprecedented efforts to exploit their vast potential. First the Lawrence company and then Murray International Metals poured money and expertise in, to buy the success that Celtic had prevented them from enjoying for a quarter of a century. It was widely assumed that the Celtic support wanted to see the same happen to their Club. Or did they? Many Celtic fans were uneasy about the direction developments were taking at Ibrox – and not simply because it looked like Rangers had at last got their act together. The relationship with business that the new financial demands on clubs dictated was something many Celtic fans instinctively resisted. Celtic was a more democratic club, more egalitarian by tradition. The thought of fat cats cornering all the best seats did not go down well with the faithful.

It also seemed that Rangers had lost their soul. David Murray was not a Rangers supporter, he was an entrepreneur. What genuine fan would have tried to buy Ayr United and be forced to sit at Somerset Park week after week?

Celtic supporters of that era would not have fancied the thought of their Club being put up for sale to the highest bidder, whether that was Trusthouse Forte or British American Tobacco. But the continuing divergence of the respective performances of the two clubs changed many minds. After five years of Rangers' victories in the League, Celtic fans would have seen their Club sold to the Ayatollah Khomeini if it gave a glimmer of hope of success on the park.

Still, in 1989 the Board was able to resist the approaches of McCann – and the many others who posed as rich men wanting to stick their fingers in the succulent Celtic pie.

What all of these people wanted was, of course, 'to help Celtic' – and control. No one came along with an offer that did not include that vital proviso. The era of talking money had arrived in overbearing fashion, seeking to oust all tradition and all links with the past. And the issue of who was to control the Club continued to dominate Celtic affairs right up to and beyond the McCann takeover.

Naturally, I felt I had a part to play in the debate and in the solution. I felt as frustrated as any fan about the way the Club was being run. I knew from my own successes in a variety of jobs that I could make a significant difference. But I wasn't myself a rich businessman able to offer financial input, and so I reckoned that my chances of getting on the Board were fairly remote. The directors didn't want any help from anyone. And they would be particularly averse to involving someone who was much better known than they were, someone who clearly had little time for the way they were running things.

But Fergus's visit convinced me that moves to take over the Club were going to be made. In order to keep control in the families, I thought I should secure some kind of a role.

I pursued this with mixed feelings. On the one hand, it must be every supporter's dream to be a director of the club he follows. On the other hand, the joy of being a fan is emotional, irrational – and unencumbered. Fans can enjoy the luxury of condemning the whole team after a bad defeat and then within seven days hailing the same players as world-beaters after an exciting victory. Directors are required to be more restrained and realistic. And realism removes the fantasy element which is football's attraction.

Chapter Three

Into a Limbo large and broad, since called
The Paradise of Fools, to few unknown.

Paradise Lost, 1.495

I remember sitting at lunch in the City Chambers in 1979 discussing the forthcoming election for Lord Provost, for which I was a leading candidate, with Labour Party colleagues. I confessed that I would rather be chairman of Celtic than win the Provostship. 'Good,' said a sharp-witted organiser for the other camp, 'You keep thinking that, because wee Neilly here is going to be Provost!' Well, I beat Neil Stobo and became the youngest Lord Provost that Glasgow had had since Patrick Colquhoun in 1732. And although that conversation was more about avoiding showing an unseemly eagerness for office – the Labour Party in Glasgow despises ambition almost as much as it suspects talent – it did indicate something about my priorities.

I was elected Lord Provost on a Thursday and one of my first official duties was to attend the Cup Final on the Saturday. It just had to be the Old Firm. Celtic won in extra time with a George McCluskey flick from a Danny McGrain shot. The Celtic crowd went mad at the end and some young fans exuberantly ran on to the field as the team headed for the Celtic end to take a bow. But Rangers supporters won't let you celebrate in peace. They had invaded Hampden once before in similar circumstances, causing the SFA temporarily to ban laps of honour. They did the same thing this time, coming on to the field to challenge the Celtic fans already there, and fights broke out all over the place.

Sitting beside me in the box was Alex Fletcher, Tory Minister for Sport. He had said very little during the game and nothing as the trouble had built up. But when the police belatedly appeared on horseback, making the situation worse if anything, he exclaimed: 'Thank Goodness for the police.' I could hardly believe what I was hearing and told him so. The trouble had developed as badly as it had precisely because at the end of the game the police patrolling the perimeter of the pitch had disappeared. One story was that they had gone to guard nearby houses against urination and vandalism. Another, nearer the truth, I suspect, was that no one had told them that this was the first final that would go to extra time if necessary, and they had simply knocked off at twenty-to-five. If they had been there in their usual numbers they could have nipped the trouble in the bud. Instead, the whole of the UK was able to witness the melodramatic sight of police horses galloping up and down Hampden. Anyway, the upshot was that I found myself for the first time on national television, defending (or rather trying to explain) the behaviour of Scottish football fans to Michael Buerk.

That was not the only incident of football controversy in my four years as Provost. Traditionally, Glasgow's Lord Provost visits each of the city's four main clubs in turn (mercifully, by then LPs were spared Queen's Park). I was horrified at having to spend Saturday afternoon at Shawfield or Firhill when Celtic were playing elsewhere. Anyway, it seemed hypocritical, everyone knew I was a Celtic supporter, why should I pretend otherwise? After the first season, Laurence Marlborough of Rangers remarked to me that he never saw me at Ibrox. 'I'm there every time Celtic play!' I told him. But, generally, Rangers took it in good part because the relationship between the two sets of directors has always been good – until recently, when Mr Murray introduced a bit of needle. When they opened their new upper deck, he was eager that all of us should marvel at it. So he went round the Boardroom, inviting the Celtic directors to take a tour. 'Rubbing it in a bit,' I said to David as he set off. So when Murray then asked me, I replied: 'No, thanks, Mr Murray. I've seen a stand.' He didn't seem too pleased.

But, of course, a Celtic-supporting LP was a recipe for a knocking story. The opportunity arose in October 1980. Rangers were playing at Hampden in the League Cup Final and Celtic had a League game at Firhill. I went to see Celtic and, as I had an official function afterwards, I went in the civic Rolls Royce. I was supposed to be back at the City Chambers for five o'clock to award the prize to the winner of a bagpiping competition and to declare him my personal piper for the year. Traffic held me up and the ceremony had to take place without me.

The Press loved it and slated me for using the official car as a supporter's bus.

I didn't think establishing my credentials so effectively with the support would do any harm to my chances of eventually becoming a director; and after a spectacularly successful spell in office, I half expected Desmond White to approach me. But he didn't.

I do not claim that I would have been the solution, but it is to this period that the decline of Celtic can be traced. Since the end of the Second World War the Club had been run by two dictatorial chairmen, Bob Kelly and Desmond White, and although Desmond was now nearing seventy no thought had been given to the succession. He had appointed his son, Christopher, to the Board in 1982 along with the commercial manager, McGinn. But Chris never wanted to be chairman, even when he had the chance to succeed McGinn in 1990. And McGinn showed no leadership whatsoever.

When Desmond died in 1984, the Club was leaderless. This vacuum led to a commercial drift that allowed external factions to build power bases from which to begin their assault on the Club. The double win in the 1988 Centenary year gave a brief respite, as did the Cup Final win over Rangers the following year. But there was no solid base.

So I had thought about the possibility of becoming a member of the Celtic Board for quite a number of years. I was, after all, a member of two of the original family dynasties. But did I really want to become involved in the inevitable stramash that surrounds Celtic? And how might it affect my business? Wouldn't it be better simply to go to the games and get on with my own life?

I toyed with these questions for months. McCann's involvement had brought the inevitablity of change to the fore. The 1990 Ne'erday game made up my mind. Rangers beat us two-nothing and the fans began to target the Board. The protests rumbled on for another four months, growing imperceptibly into a campaign. The fans, like hungry sheep, looked up and were not fed their diet of success. I watched at every home and away game as the directors seemed deaf to the sentiments and blind to the dangers. Back in my office, my staff were beginning to notice my restlessness and anxiety. I paced the floor trying to think of a way to get myself elected to the Board.

The fans' protests reached a climax on 30 March 1990 when Motherwell beat us two-one at Celtic Park. It was an occasion when I had offered my own box for the day to a senior member of my staff, Mike Stanger. A cricketer whose only previous attendance at a football match had been twenty years earlier (also at Celtic Park for a match against Aberdeen), Mike filled the box with personal acquaintances and fellow cricketers – all, he claimed, potential clients! During the second half, fans began making rude and offensive chants about Jack McGinn. After the game, they gathered in the car park outside for half an hour to chant 'Sack the Board' – words that were to become depressingly familiar over the next four years. But when I first heard them, I was an outsider looking in. And Mike Stanger and his cricketing friends were utterly nonplussed.

In my opinion, the only person on the Board at that time with the necessary ability was Chris White. In addition to having a BA from Strathclyde University, Chris was a qualified and practising CA. I had been as close as anybody to Desmond, his father – which nevertheless meant light-years from properly knowing this powerful and strange individual. He and I shared an interest in scuba diving, and in the late 1970s I went on a trip to Dornoch to dive with him. It gave me the chance to study this enigmatic individual, who had such a strong influence on the Club. My clearest memory is of discussing Einstein's Theory of Relativity with him over dinner. He couldn't quite remember the simple model of the light on the moving train which most easily illustrates the principle of time depending on speed. But the next morning at breakfast he came down with an envelope, on the back of which he had a wee drawing which made the point.

Anyway, I knew Chris quite well. But not well enough to ask him straight for a seat on the Board. I bumped into him outside Love Street before a game early in 1990 and broached the subject of a change of direction. Not surprisingly, he had given the matter a lot of thought. He had concluded that, unless change came from within, it would be enforced by outside pressures. He saw the need for new directors and cautiously hinted that I might be among the candidates.

Things proceeded slowly over the next few months. Then, in March 1990, Francis McCrossin (a distinguished Glasgow CA), Brian Dempsey (a client of Farrell's), David Smith and I were interviewed by the Board. I trailed up to the offices of Shaughnessy, Quigley and McColl (Farrell's law firm) to subject myself to inane questioning from people I spoke to about Celtic at every game. Chris would break no confidences, so I never found out exactly how the discussions went, but it was clear from the long delay before anything was heard that the Board really wanted no additions at all. They were determined to soldier on.

To break the deadlock, a deal was done between Chris and Farrell. If Chris would support Dempsey's appointment, Farrell would vote for me. And that's what happened. On 30 April 1990, the Board agreed that Dempsey and I should join and we were co-opted on 3 May.

The media gave us an ecstatic welcome. Dempsey was hailed as the man to bring business acumen to the Club. I was regarded as the PR guru, fresh from my 'Glasgow's Miles Better' campaign, equipped to rally the Celtic faithful from around the globe. But whereas Dempsey was seen as a break from the tradition, my appointment was just that of another member of the 'families' who had controlled Celtic since 1888. I was therefore regarded – right from the beginning – as a member of the old guard.

Nevertheless, I was determined to make the best of the good public relations send-off which greeted our appointment, and genuinely wanted to work in tandem with Dempsey to achieve what seemed to me our joint objectives. I assumed that we were now part of the Boardroom 'team'. But a small incident the day after our appointment was a portent of things to come.

Charged with the task of co-ordinating the Club's publicity, I offered the *Evening Times* an exclusive picture of Dempsey and me, and I had my graphics designer produce a 'Celtic's Miles Better' slogan in the style of the famous Glasgow one. I could have posed for the picture by myself, but it never occurred to me that I might have done that until after Dempsey arrived. He displayed a baffling coolness towards the idea, but reluctantly agreed to the picture being taken. The picture was splashed across the front page of the *Evening Times*, so it was clear the idea was sound.

Our co-option to the Board was in time for us to go to the Cup Final as directors. Traditionally, Celtic directors go into dressing room just before a big game to wish the players luck. Visiting the players then was the part of the job that I enjoyed most. This was the heart of the Club and where every fan would want to be, joining in the last-minute nerves, hearing the final tactical instructions, shouting the words of encouragement. In all my time as a director, I always looked forward to coming straight off the team bus and walking into the dressing room with the players – for a minute only, then Neilly Mochan chased us all out so that he could hang up the strips. I then used to walk out on to the pitch with the rest of the team.

Fans who turn up an hour early must be used to the sight of the visiting team inspecting the pitch. I could never figure out what the inspection was all about. So when I became part of it myself, I asked the players what we were doing out there, especially on cold wet Scottish Saturdays. I got some murmurs about 'checking the conditions' or 'seeing if the grass took a stud'. But none were very convincing. Then it dawned on me. We were out there so that Neilly could have room to unpack the kit! Given the size of some dressing rooms (Tynecastle, which shrunk visibly over the years, springs first to mind), he needed the solitude.

Billy McNeill was always very tolerant of me in the dressing room, seeing how much I enjoyed being a part of things. I am afraid that I sometimes overstayed my visit. Players and manager do need time to themselves in the last half hour before the game, as the manager counts the time down to focus attention. But I wanted to learn something of the secret of football management. Billy had been one of Celtic's most successful managers. How did he do it? What was the key to motivation? I am afraid that my conclusions are not very profound. It seems to me that this type of management is an innate gift, depending so much on personality rather than on learned techniques.

Liam Brady was more sensitive. He really didn't like the directors being in the dressing room. Before the EUFA Cup-tie against Cologne in Germany, he sent a message through Terry Cassidy that, as it was such an important game, he didn't want any director coming into the dressing room. His wishes were respected – but it didn't make any difference, because after an appalling performance against a poor team we lost two-nothing.

It has been a long tradition that, on the team bus, the manager and the directors sit at the front with the team at the back. Cassidy thought this was bad management: 'They're Brady's lads. He should be sitting with them. I would.' And he told Liam so.

That night of the Cologne defeat was the night when, driving back with the team to the airport, Grant and I got very annoyed at the sound of players laughing and joking with each other. We were both extremely depressed at the way we had played and could see no cause for amusement. In fact, if it hadn't been for the iron rule that the directors never, ever, interfered with team matters, I would have stood up on the bus and told a few of them what I thought of their attitude to a defeat. Liam, on the other hand, was upset that the directors (he meant me and Grant) were walking around the airport with long faces, making our displeasure obvious to the players and management team. I sat down beside him for a talk. Players know when they have played badly, he argued. The fact that they may be having a laugh a couple of hours later is no indication that they were not taking a reversal seriously. Directors looking miserable didn't help anybody.

I suppose that it comes down to different views of management, because I certainly didn't agree with him. Modern players get very large carrots to enjoy: a bit of psychological stick at the right time must be part of the package. If you appear not to care, then onlookers might be justified in concluding that you don't care. Whatever the principle, in this case Liam had the last laugh because we won the second leg at Celtic Park three-nothing and went into the draw for the next round.

An exception to the non-interference rule was an incident when I saw bottles and cans of beer being brought on to the bus for the players. I questioned George Douglas, the Operations Executive, as to the legal position. He wasn't sure, so I told him to check and let me know the next day. He confirmed that it was against the law. I told him that he should inform Liam and have it stopped. Innocuous though it was, it would not do for it to become known that the Club was ignoring a very sensitive issue.

Given this happened in 1993, I was surprised when I read that one of the things Macari was being criticised for at the time of his dismissal was allowing beer on the bus. The practice had been going on long before his appointment.

Anyway, back to Hampden and the Cup Final. Billy introduced Dempsey and me to the players as two new directors. Then he invited us to say something. Now, I am as good as anyone at making impromptu speeches. In the right circumstances, just try to stop me. But here, I didn't think it right that I should say anything at all. I didn't want to upset the delicate and detailed preparations that had been gone through to bring the players to a peak of concentration. I could imagine how I would have felt a few minutes before an exam having to listen to some words of ponderous advice. Again, these players were my heroes. Director or not, I was merely a supporter. What could I say that would inspire them? I said nothing.

Dempsey delivered a speech.

There was no scoring during the game or the extra time. Then, on the last penalty to be taken by an outfield player, Anton Rogan missed and Aberdeen scored to make Celtic the first team to lose the Scottish Cup on penalties.

I came back into a miserable dressing room to share the pain. McNeill's first remark ' . . . that awful feeling . . .' reminded me that he had experienced failure as a player before Stein's arrival. It was clear that the hatred of defeat as well as the joy of victory was what had helped make his success. Then he said: 'I wish it had been anyone other than Anton. He'll take it worse than anybody.'

I went back to Celtic Park with the team. It was a silent bus until we turned from Springfield Road into London Road and Packie Bonner began quietly singing the Celtic song and we all joined in, almost in tears. Then I saw two fans standing outside the chip shop at the lights waving their scarves in salute and felt even sadder.

A post-match meal had been laid on in the Walfrid, basically to feed the players. It was now six o'clock and they had last eaten at twelve. It was a drab, dismal affair, much worse than any wake I have attended. Then, towards the end, Billy came round every table instructing everyone to lift their heads. 'That's enough. We've suffered the pain, now we've got to look ahead.'

I'd seen McNeill in victory for many years. This insight into how he handled defeat showed his qualities as a person and as a manager. It was behaviour like that which made me hesitate for so long over his removal, and which led me to suggest at the Board meeting which sacked him that he should be given a role. That's why I later said on television that I thought there should be a place for him at Celtic Park. Why the Press decided that that was a controversial proposal, I'll never know, because I still think he would be of immeasurable value to the Club, especially now with so few Celtic people running things.

On the way out of the Park, I bumped into Dempsey. Exchanging the usual mutual commiserations that Celtic supporters all over Scotland were engaged in, he said: 'Ach, it's not the end of the world.' I was horrified. Of course it was!

Chapter Four

What reinforcement we may gain from hope,
If not, what resolution from despair . . . .

Paradise Lost, 1.190

The new Board set about tackling the problems, the biggest
one of which was perceived to be the stadium issue. Dempsey
claimed to be the expert on this, and the Press duly acclaimed
his expertise. In fact, though he had a background in property, it
was mainly in private house-building. It was pretty clear, even to
a non-expert, that the redevelopment of Celtic Park was unlikely
to be financially viable or to provide a physically satisfactory
solution.

Celtic Park, when regarded as a property investment, had
always been in the wrong part of Glasgow. Despite the best
efforts of the last Labour government's Scottish Development
Agency, the East End has remained derelict and depressed. There
is still little demand for commercial and industrial land. The
successful development of the adjacent Parkhead Forge Retail
Centre had pre-empted the only possible ancillary activity to
a revamped Celtic Park. Another shopping complex simply
wouldn't receive planning permission, even if a developer could
be found who believed that it could make money in such close
proximity to a successful rival. So there was no possibility of
selling Celtic Park for 'planning gain' to boost the finance
available for a new stadium.

The Parkhead site itself is bounded to the north by Janefield
Street and the cemetery beyond. The only way of building a
decent-sized stand to replace the Jungle is to move the pitch
towards the main stand, removing a number of the front
rows. Innumerable feasibility studies were done by engineers
and architects, who were otherwise twiddling their thumbs
during the recession. All demonstrated that such modifications
would physically be possible, though how satisfactory was

open to question. But the financial plans indicated that there was no chance of the repayments on the investment required, estimated variously from £15 to £35 million, being recovered from the increased revenues generated. Even the most optimistic assumptions about the sale of seat debentures, which had been disastrous for so many English clubs, could not bridge the gap. It was obvious that the best physical solution involved moving to another site. There were plenty of candidates – from Renfrewshire Enterprise's Linwood Park to an audacious scheme to reverse conventional wisdom and build a city centre stadium on the site of the old High Street railway goods yard.

The Board had been aware of the option of leaving Celtic Park long before I became a director. Their deliberations culminated with a full-day session in the Hospitality Inn in Glasgow in February 1990 when various options were considered. Among the names in contention at that time were Bovis, Fairhurst, British Aerospace and Lovell.

Meanwhile, I was trying to come up with a sensible public relations plan for Celtic. Some people had expected me to undertake some sort of world tour, drumming up expatriate Celtic supporters to part with tranches of money to enable the Club to build a new stadium and buy a new team. I never saw that as a realistic task. When I was Lord Provost of Glasgow, I went on such a trip on behalf of the city. Much though I was fêted wherever I went, particularly in North America and Australasia, I never formed the impression that the world was populated by rich Celts eager to be separated from their money. But I did feel that I could put Celtic's public relations on a much more professional basis.

The usual routine in my firm whenever we prepared a pitch to present to a firm seeking PR advice was to brainstorm ideas with one or more of our account executives. In this case, I had a ready-made football fan working for me, and one with an impeccable Celtic name, John Thomson. But, although John contributed ideas to our presentation, I thought it would be a good idea if we brought a completely fresh mind to the task, one with no preconceived ideas about football in general, or Celtic in particular. So I asked Mike Stanger, a former senior BBC producer, to draft our proposal document.

As part of the fact-finding exercise, I suggested that Mike speak to each of the directors in turn, which he did, discovering for himself the full and often contradictory range of opinions about the Club which existed within the Boardroom. He also gave the utmost independent thought to what seemed to be required at Celtic Park. His report included the following comments and advice:

> The media acquire information about Celtic from a wide variety of sources, including 'rumour' and 'invention'! Indeed, some journalists seem to regard it as being entirely unnecessary to speak to anyone from the club when writing about it . . . Journalists expressed dissatisfaction with the way their enquiries are dealt with . . .
>
> There is a general feeling among the businessmen who support Celtic financially that the club is not customer-friendly . . . to put it bluntly, they would say that the club has an attitude problem . . . It is an area which must be tackled as a matter of urgency . . .
>
> The starting point must be to establish how Celtic sees itself and what image it wants to portray of itself . . . Celtic is much more than a business, and much more than a football club. It is not the establishment club. It is not the club of big business. It is much more the family club. It is the People's Club. Celtic has a heart, a soul, a conscience. No Scottish club has a greater right to claim a place in the top leagues. But it believes that these developments must spring from the existing organisation in Scotland and not in any break-away attempts . . .

Mike's recommendations included a revamp of the *Celtic View*; improvements in the Club's media relations, on the playing side as well as corporately; the appointment of a single non-football Club spokesperson; a proactive media stance; a fresh, professionally co-ordinated corporate design; a 'Celtic Goes Green' environmentally-friendly policy; a major commercial effort; and improved staff communications. In a later, separate memo, we recommended the appointment 'in due course' of an in-house public relations officer, to carry out the daily grind of nitty-gritty media and public relations.

I thought it was an excellent report, full of detailed insight. But, although some of the ideas in the report were tried out later in the Cassidy era, the Board weren't overly impressed by the need for PR improvements. The lack of a formal system in many ways suited the individual directors who could gain media exposure as and when they felt like it. The last thing that they wanted was the creation of one spokesperson whose existence would effectively gag them.

In the event, because of the dramas which are described in this book, the whole issue became entangled with the various personalities. As a Board, we never got to grips with the PR problem from start to finish. The number of occasions when either Terry Cassidy, or Grant, or Kevin took the rest of us completely by surprise with premature, unauthorised or damaging public statements were all too numerous ... and many of them had crucial bearings on our fortunes, as I will demonstrate.

Above all, any football club's image depends crucially on its results. If the team is toiling on the field, the media reflect the fans' unhappiness by criticising everything about the club, not just the playing side. During the 'nine-in-a-row' years, when Rangers were failing to get results, their directors were mercilessly harassed by the media. In Celtic's case, when you add to the poor performance an insidious and deliberate campaign of destabilisation by a group desperate for control, the public relations problem becomes a nightmare – and, indeed, is probably incapable of solution. Until results improve.

But my main concern at this time, besides the PR task, was that we should settle the stadium issue. As the summer went on, Dempsey began to push harder and harder for a move to Robroyston. The site had a controversial history. It was the former Robroyston Hospital and had a chequered past, even before being acquired by an Aberdeen firm, Jaymarke Ltd, with whom Dempsey claimed to have had previous dealings. He proposed a major development on the site, with the stadium supplemented by a hotel, a retail park, a petrol station and housing. Celtic would enter into a joint venture with Jaymarke and apply for planning permission. When this was granted, Celtic would acquire ownership of 60 acres on which to build a stadium, and would receive a share of any profits from the whole development.

These proposals were incorporated in three draft legal agreements which Dempsey presented to the Board for approval. The first was the Joint Venture Agreement. Under this, Celtic and Jaymarke would agree to become shareholders in another company called Bernlaw Ltd, set up on 13 June 1993, to pursue their interest in the Robroyston site.

The objects of Bernlaw were to buy the site from Jaymarke, to obtain planning permission for the proposed developments and to sell all or part of the site at a profit. Celtic were to be 24% shareholders in the venture, with Jaymarke taking 74% and the right to take up or sell the remaining 2% of the equity. There were to be two directors nominated by each shareholder. If Jaymarke sold the 2% of the equity outstanding, it could nominate a further director to represent the purchaser. As Celtic would have had no say in who the purchaser might be, Jaymarke therefore would effectively have controlled both the shareholding and the board of Bernlaw. The registered office of the company was to be in Aberdeen, with Aberdeen accountants as auditors. Jaymarke would conduct the 'general financial management' of the company and charge for so doing.

Initially, the agreement required both Celtic and Jaymarke to make available to Bernlaw interest-free loans of £625,000. And both would 'contribute equally such further sums' as Bernlaw decided were necessary. If Celtic refused, or were unable to do so, it was spelt out that Jaymarke could sue. Within 15 days, Bernlaw had to buy the Robroyston site from Jaymarke for £2.5 million.

So, for a contribution of £625,000, Jaymarke would get £1.25 million from Celtic for a site which they had bought for much less years previously. And, in any circumstances whatsoever, further calls could be made on capital sums from Celtic, for any purpose whether directly connected with the proposed stadium or not. It did not seem an equitable arrangement to me, nor to Chris White. But the rest of the Celtic Board, bringing all their accumulated experience of the property world to bear, were ecstatic about the prospects of the Dempsey dream scheme.

The principle, of course, was right. Celtic needed to get away from Parkhead. Celtic needed to build a new stadium. Celtic needed a related commercial development to make the whole scheme viable. To that extent, Dempsey's dream was admirably conceived.

But there were three areas where it failed the test of being a practical, commercially viable proposal. First, the joint venture agreement severely disadvantaged Celtic. Secondly, the details of how the project was to be financed were worryingly woolly. There was no apparent financial plan: the only element of the financing of the project seemed to be 'planning gain', an unquantifiable concept which would give the Club a bit of money along with the 'free' land on which to build the stadium. How the stadium itself would be financed was never explained despite repeated requests for it to be spelt out. Thirdly, there appeared to be little prospect of planning permission being obtained.

All of these questions loomed large in Chris's mind. He and I voiced them, repeatedly, at Board meetings. The answers were urbane, as usual, long on glib reassurance but desperately short of serious detail. We kept being reminded that Dempsey was the property expert, and we had to take his word for it that everything would be OK. Eventually, because of the delays caused by our concern, he himself took up the option with Jaymarke by using another of his companies, Strathvale Holdings, whose interest in Robroyston he said he would transfer to Celtic if we agreed to go to Robroyston.

Meanwhile, I pursued the question of planning permission. It seemed that it would be unlikely to be granted. The site was in the green belt and the mooted office, retail and hotel developments breached Strathclyde Region's structure plan and other planning strictures. I phoned Jimmy Rae, Glasgow's Director of Planning, to get an informed view. He told me quite bluntly that the chances of any such scheme gaining consent were remote. He would oppose all the developments broadly described as commercial. He would recommend the housing for approval because the Secretary of State perceived there was a shortage of housing land in Glasgow and would not necessarily object to the green belt being breached. He might also approve the planned stadium – but he would not approve both the housing and the stadium together, because he regarded them as incompatible uses.

So, that was pretty clear. We would probably get planning permission for a stadium, but all the other elements of the development, all the items which might produce planning gain, essential to begin its funding, would be refused. I reported this to the Board.

But, of course, that was just the District's view. There is an appeal process which a developer can use to take the final decision right up to the Secretary of State for Scotland. But, on deeper investigation, I discovered another reason why the project was unlikely to come to fruition in the way Dempsey had described. Much of the land at that time was farmland – and agricultural leases are the firmest there are. The lease-holder in this case was none other than Glasgow District Council, the planning authority. So, even if an appeal to the Secretary of State had been successful, the District's permission to build the development would still be required. Given Jimmy Rae's opinion that the application would be opposed, it seemed to me unlikely that they would remove their objection.

Despite this, and the fact that on 9 July 1990 the Board agreed to allow Bovis to conduct a feasibility study for both the development of Celtic Park and a new stadium on a greenfield site, Dempsey pushed Robroyston harder and harder. When Farrell and I were guests of his in Italy for the World Cup, we met a planning official with Glasgow District Council, who explained Robroyston issues. I was so worried about what was said that I reported the matter to Jimmy Rae when I came back to Glasgow.

On 25 June 1990 the Board was asked to consider the Robroyston scheme. On 26 July 1990 the joint venture and development agreements were tabled for the first time. Despite the fact that Kevin and I were both absent, Dempsey asked the Board to come to a decision right away. Farrell backed him. And Grant and McGinn, who had previously wanted the redevelopment of Celtic Park, now went for the greenfield site option.

Dempsey spoke for the move, arguing that 'he did not have the same sentimental attachment to the existing stadium as other directors might have'. He dismissed the idea that Celtic Park could be effectively re-developed.

Chris was less concerned with sentiment than with the practicalities of the move. He wanted to wait for the recently-commissioned Bovis feasibility study: why commission it, and then press ahead without waiting for its conclusions? Dempsey became impatient and said he was used to making quicker decisions than Chris apparently could. But Chris thought the matter so important and far-reaching that he wanted to put it before the shareholders. This would mean an EGM which Farrell did not think was 'technically required'. Chris refused to be rushed and insisted on postponing a decision until his return from holiday.

When I heard of this discussion, I too felt that we were being railroaded into a decision on an unsound project without any proper analysis. There was no estimate of how a new stadium on a remote site could be financed. As there was no estimate of how a refurbishment of Celtic Park could be paid for, it was not possible to compare Robroyston with it, far less other possible sites, except in the most general of ways. How could it possibly be sensible to make a multi-million pound decision in that state of ignorance?

On 14 August 1990 I argued that, before any decision was made, we should investigate fully the feasibility of re-developing Celtic Park. We should then assess this in comparison with the merits of a number of different sites. I also urged the Board that we should approach the Scottish Football Association to explore the possibility of a joint development. And I emphasised that, before we made any commitments, the funding implications of any investment, whether at Celtic Park or elsewhere, had to be fully and professionally investigated.

Sadly, contributions like that to the Boardroom debates were regarded as mere filibustering. It was made out that Chris and I were opposing Robroyston because of some personality clash with Dempsey. The Board thought that they had been considering the stadium question for nearly two years and were desperate to move on and make a decision. Of course, they hadn't considered anything. They had merely been hearing about the same thing again and again – no one knew what proper assessment was, so they certainly weren't capable of making it. Every question I put appeared simply to be another delaying tactic.

On 13 September 1990 another Board meeting was held, this time in the Albany Hotel, to review eight options: redeveloping Celtic Park, sharing Hampden, or building new at Strathclyde Park, Molendinar, Cambuslang, London Road (British Steel) site, Robroyston or Easterhouse. But the review was a superficial one: there simply was not enough information available to make a considered judgement. The Board were going through the motions.

At this meeting, the real possibility of Celtic co-operating with the SFA to build and share a new national stadium emerged.

McGinn was authorised to meet the office-bearers of the SFA to pursue this. He reported back on 20 September 1990 that he had met office-bearers of the SFA and that 'they were positive on the idea of sharing a national stadium with Celtic'.

The momentum for Robroyston continued to build relentlessly. But, with the genuine concern which had been expressed, when Chris proposed that a second legal opinion be sought on the terms of the Bernlaw and Jaymarke agreements presented by Dempsey, the Board readily agreed. Farrell undertook to arrange it, and to choose the lawyers best suited to the task. The choice was his and his alone, and he chose one of Scotland's top three legal firms.

In the middle of all the woolliness about the financial plan for a £50 million stadium project, Dempsey managed to find time to be quite precise about other financial matters. During the Board meeting on 22 July 1990, only three weeks after he took his seat, he was going on at his usual length about 'grasping the commercial opportunities' and 'bringing the club into the modern world'. Suddenly, he asked what the executive directors were paying themselves. The answers were: McGinn £25,000, Chris £20,000 and Grant £18,000. 'Ridiculous,' pronounced Dempsey, 'I move they should be doubled.' Though startled by the suggestion and modest in their self-assessment, eventually the directors agreed to increase the executive salaries to £40,000, £30,000 and – because Farrell insisted on removing the differential between Chris and Grant – £30,000 respectively. The ad hoc way in which this was done was wrong. Any review of executive directors' salaries is normally conducted solely by the non-executive directors, who then make a recommendation to the whole Board. Specifically, I thought it was odd to spend another £37,000 a year for no extra return at all. But when someone is throwing around largesse, even if it's not his own, it is difficult to be the spoilsport. I was wrong not to register my dissent. The story leaked out, naturally, after Dempsey left the Board, generating further bad publicity – but not for Dempsey, who wasn't mentioned.

I returned from a holiday break in Istanbul in early October 1990, to find that the solicitors appointed by Farrell had, while I was away, written two letters to the Board. The Board considered one of these letters at its meeting of 20 September 1990, and the other at a meeting on 4 October 1990.

The solicitors confirmed that they had read the Joint Venture Agreement, the Supplementary Agreement and the Development Agreement involving Celtic, Strathvale Holdings and Jaymarke, and that they were concerned about aspects of what was proposed. Indeed, they recommended that the best way forward was to scrap the existing documents and start again.

They first confirmed what Chris had thought, namely that an EGM would be necessary before the project could go ahead. The Board could not approve it without first changing Celtic's Memorandum and Articles of Association.

The areas of concern which they highlighted were:

1. The equity issue: while Celtic were to hold only 25% of the shares [that is, 25% of the 98% to be issued], and therefore only 25% of any dividends, the Club would be bound to contribute 50% of the initial interest-free loan of £1.25 million and any future cash calls.

   • It was not clear whether the guarantees were open-ended or not. And it was not clear how any proceeds would be split.

   • The Club would be responsible for 50% of any shortfalls or lack of finance.

   • If Jaymarke were to manage the project (and that was the intention), they would be paid for so doing. Their position of control would allow them to fix their own remuneration.

   • Although Celtic's 'reward' was to be a 'free' site, this would only be triggered by the granting of planning permission for not only the stadium, but also everything else in the scheme. Furthermore, in the unlikely event of everything else but the stadium being approved, the land still wouldn't be given to Celtic.

   • Jaymarke would be entitled to 75% of the enhanced value of the stadium site after planning permission had been obtained. (So, if the undeveloped site 'given' to Celtic had been worth £1 million, for example, and planning gain had raised its value to £4 million, Celtic could finally acquire the 'free' site by paying Jaymarke £3 million!)

2. The open-ended nature of the commitments.

3. Celtic's right to sell on all or part of its interests in the development were limited. In particular, the Club would still have to guarantee that the obligations of the purchaser were honoured. Jaymarke, on the other hand, could assign one-third of its interest without Celtic's agreement, and without the kind of guarantee being asked of Celtic.

The second letter from the independent solicitors chosen by Farrell responded to the Board's request for guidance, and contained policy as well as legal advice. They first posed the fundamental question as to whether or not the Board was 'prepared to become involved in a development scheme of a speculative nature with inherent potential benefits and risks to Celtic'?

The letter expected the answer to be 'no', but added that, if it was 'yes', a further question arose: was the Board prepared simply to adopt the agreements in their present form or did they wish to try to improve on the conditions – and, if so, how far were Celtic prepared to go? The solicitors took the view that 'there are certain basic adjustments required to the Documentation before Celtic can comfortably become involved ... in short, we cannot recommend that Celtic simply adopts the Documentation at this stage without at least an attempt to improve on its terms from Celtic's point of view: the risk is too great.'

Their advice on how to proceed was clear:

1. Jaymarke should be told that Celtic was taking advice on the proposed agreements.

2. Jaymarke should be told that the Club needed more time in which to make their decisions about the proposals.

3. While the Board as a whole needed to agree the 'end position', a negotiating group quite separate from those who had hitherto been involved in the discussions with Jaymarke should conduct the re-negotiations about the conditions of the proposed agreements.

And they recommended 'firmly' that Celtic should engage the services of a professional property adviser to advise on the valuation aspects of the agreements. 'It will not do for Celtic to be negotiating this kind of transaction without independent property advice. That advice is fundamental to the quantification of potential downside to Celtic and the assessment of the strength of Celtic's negotiating position. We do not think that Mr Dempsey can properly fill this role as we remain concerned at the potential conflict of interest between Celtic and Strathvale. But, in any event, Mr Dempsey by his own admission is not experienced in commercial property matters, his expertise being in residential development.'

As Celtic's core business was not property development, the solicitors recommended that the Club's 'exposure to risk should be limited to the absolute minimum acceptable to Jaymarke/Strathvale'. While this might limit the benefits to the Club, they felt that this was 'preferable to Celtic being fully exposed in the way the Documentation presently contemplates'. The solicitors also felt that the funding of the stadium building costs had not been properly considered.

Finally, they identified 'one delicate issue . . . the clear conflict at present between the respective interests of Strathvale and Celtic. Mr Dempsey's role seems to us to be quite pivotal at the moment in that he considers Strathvale are simply holding a position in the development concept which Celtic may or may not elect to take up. As we have tried to illustrate in this letter, it is not that simple and indeed one scenario which we think the Board should explore is whether there is a way forward on a tripartite basis with Jaymarke and Strathvale fulfilling the speculative roles and Celtic (on the back of the planning benefit they are bringing to the table) acquiring their new stadium site with no or very little downside risk. Clearly Celtic and Strathvale require to be separately advised when considering their own positions and this has already been addressed from a legal point of view with Messrs Jno Shaughnessy Quigley & McColl acting for Strathvale and us acting for Celtic. The added difficulty we perceive is how to avoid compromising the positions of Celtic and/or Strathvale without losing the benefit of Mr Dempsey's undoubted expertise in this matter as well as his background knowledge. We think this matter needs to be considered further by the Board.'

I read the lawyers' opinions with horror at the realisation that Celtic could have been committed to a potentially ruinous deal. Every doubt which Chris and I had expressed had been picked up and amplified with expertise and authority. Their conclusions were unequivocal: the Robroyston deal was not a good one for Celtic, the Board would be putting the Club at risk by agreeing it. Naïvely, I assumed that on reading these papers the Board would ditch the Robroyston scheme without demur, or at the very least seek the re-negotiation the lawyers advised. How wrong I was.

The second letter from our solicitors was considered on 4 October 1990, but the reaction of the other directors was not what I had anticipated. McGinn considered the letter to be 'jaundiced' and 'overstepping the terms of reference'. Kevin 'was not happy' with it. Grant supported them. Dempsey went further. He 'considered it insulting and was seeking legal opinion as to whether it was actionable'.

While I was expecting Dempsey to defend his scheme, the reaction of the others left me nonplussed. The solicitors' warnings were crystal clear and I was looking for the Board to recognise that what Chris and I had been arguing had been proved correct. Instead, it was obvious that their minds were set on adopting Robroyston and that all independent advice to the contrary was to be rubbished.

After the meeting, Chris and I discussed the situation. We now despaired of stopping Robroyston. If the Board would not see sense, we would be powerless to prevent the Club from getting entangled in a financially dangerous contractual relationship, which would have turned the Club into property developers with an open-ended commitment to fund the scheme. Celtic wasn't being run properly. The Club was even less well equipped to manage this.

Then I received an astonishing and brave phone call to my office. It was from Nick Farrell, Jimmy's son, a senior and experienced chartered surveyor with Chesterton's, one of the foremost property agents in Britain. Nick was himself a Celtic shareholder, and told me he was professionally concerned about the Robroyston scheme, and he had written to his father about his concerns. He undertook to provide me with a copy of his two-page memo of 4 September 1990 to his father. It posed the professional's genuine misgivings about the venture – and it was from an objective source. He had also examined the proposed agreements, which led him to make observations and to ask questions such as:

- Why, when the parties are putting up cash in equal shares, should Jaymarke get the lion's share of the profits?

- Why is a football club exposing itself to such commitment when the proper business of the club has absolutely nothing to do with property development? What if the joint developer goes into receivership? Is there not total exposure to any outstanding loans, etc.?

- The site is not quite 'free' if there is need to pay for the cost of a link road. Is there an estimate for what this road will cost? What if the planners insist on a dual carriageway for the industrial/business park development, do Jaymarke then pay for additional cost? What are the ground conditions here? A link road to dual carriageway standard is a very expensive business. It could run into millions of pounds. If this is a joint venture and the link road is very much of benefit to Jaymarke, why not at very worst 50/50 or 75/25 in the Club's favour like everything else? This is definitely a very dangerous situation.

- What have Jaymarke got to do with the Club development? They are making no financial contribution. This is completely unnecessary and unwise.

- If the Club sells the site at any time in the future for any other use other than stated then Jaymarke get 75% of the sale price. This is totally unfair. Does the original contribution of £625,000 get deducted in the first instance? This agreed split is totally unfair from the Club point of view.

- Do the Club intend to give up control of the company by allowing Jaymarke to appoint a fifth director and to have a controlling vote thus throwing away any form of democracy?

- Surely it would be very unwise to have all financial handlings of the company's affairs dealt with by Jaymarke?

- This potentially means draining the Club of further financial resources in order to achieve 'the objectives' of the agreement. What if Jaymarke have control of the company?

- If the Club defaults, the other party can force it to sell its shares at a value to be fixed by Ernst & Young (independent CAs). This seems totally unacceptable.

- 'The reserved shares' – what are these? Where have they come

44

from? Is it not at this point that Jaymarke take over the Board? The Club have two directors, Jaymarke have three.

• Who pays what? How much more money are Celtic committed to? Is it 25%? Why?

• Is this not dangerous ground in a situation where the majority shareholder is in control of the day-to-day running of a company? Could the other party not be the recipient of immediate cash calls? Could this not be very dangerous?

• Does this not mean that the Club would be participating in construction and development including taking large sums on loan at 50/50 share to get a 25% share of profit? This is in no way the business of the Club. Do Jaymarke want the Club to be involved or is the Club seen as a nuisance?

Nick Farrell added that it appeared to him that the Club could be in very serious trouble if Jaymarke were to go bust during construction works: 'Many have suffered this fate recently.'

He was also clearly worried that the site was not being offered 'free' to the Club: 'It will cost the Club the additional cost of the link road (£1m++?), then the ball starts rolling. The Club are further committed to £625,000 (or is it £1.25m?). Potentially you have a site to start costing £2.25m. Once development starts – and remember this not only applies to a new stadium – then cash calls on the Club would be immediate and over which they may have no control. If the Club then defaulted and did not pay up, Jaymarke would force the Club to sell its shares in the company at a price to be determined not by an independent arbiter but by the company's auditors. (What did Jaymarke pay for the site, anyway?) When will planning permission be obtained for the development over which Jaymarke have control as to content, lodging dates and approval times? And, during this period of capital lock-up, how would the Club progress the building of a stadium? I thought Jaymarke wanted the Club as a catalyst? Is the Club a developer?'

Nick Farrell thought the whole project could take years to come to fruition. He also understood ground conditions on the site were very poor. Then his final summary: 'The Club could end up in a position where they have no control, are locked into a minority position on a board, have to do what Jaymarke say and have to take account of Jaymarke's views on the Club's business. If the venture fails, the Club will have to make good the position on the monies and in the event that Jaymarke disappear. This venture has the hallmark of great risk attached to it and is not recommended.'

My own objections to the weaknesses in the proposed agreement with Jaymarke forced McGinn and Grant to travel to Aberdeen to see if they could get them eliminated. They met the two directors with whom Dempsey had been dealing, Alan Wilson and James Shaw. But they didn't get very far.

Jaymarke would not agree that the trigger for Celtic to get the stadium site should be 'planning permission for the stadium in isolation'. They insisted on full planning permission for everything in the application. The two directors seemed to accept the reassurance that Jaymarke 'would not abuse the wording'. After seeking a ceiling on Celtic's obligations, all McGinn and Grant could report was that Jaymarke did not want either party 'to be involved in further expenditure other than the planning costs which could be in the region of £100,000'. They adamantly refused to budge from the position that Celtic would have only 25% of the equity while being responsible for 50% of the costs.

Nick Farrell also came to me with information about some recent changes in land ownership at Robroyston, and supplied me with the supporting documentary evidence of his researches. He had discovered that a number of small pockets of land within the areas earmarked for the housing development parts of the overall scheme had been registered in the name of Nardlaw Ltd, an off-the-shelf company jointly formed and owned by Jaymarke and SL Homes Ltd. SL Homes Ltd was a housing development company. On 2 February 1989, 49% of the shares were allotted to Brian Dempsey and 49% to Bothwell Management Services – a company associated with the Scottish Legal Life Assurance Company.

Nardlaw Ltd was incorporated on 26 July 1990. On 17 August 1990, 49% of the shares in Nardlaw were allotted to SL Homes Ltd and 49% to Jaymarke. Alan Wilson and James Shaw (the directors of Jaymarke), Harry Millar of Scottish Legal Life Assurance Society and Brian Dempsey were made directors. On the same day, the objects clause of Nardlaw was changed to turn it into a property company.

Faced with this from Nick Farrell, I decided to take legal advice about my personal responsibilities as a Celtic director. I consulted W & J Burness, who were specialists in company law.

I was concerned that the other members of the Board did not know of Dempsey's potential interest in the development (other than on behalf of Celtic and Strathvale Holdings); that the Board had not properly considered other development schemes; and that the Board had failed to take advice from any suitably qualified property adviser and, indeed, seemed unwilling to take the advice which it had received from its solicitors.

Burness's letter to me of 22 October 1990 was explicit and instructive. First they confirmed that, on 27 September 1990, two dealings were registered in respect of land at Robroyston in the Land Register. One of the dealings transferred some land to Jaymarke and the other transferred three plots to Nardlaw Ltd.

They confirmed what I already knew, that my overriding duty was to the shareholders of Celtic, and that the best interests of the company as a whole should be actively pursued over and above the personal interests of any director, including myself.

They told me explicitly that I had 'a duty to bring Mr Dempsey's apparent interests and potential conflict of interest to the attention of the other members of the Board and, indeed, to allow Mr Dempsey to explain if he considers that no conflict of interest arises'.

They also advised me to insist that the Board, in order to protect the position of all the directors took proper professional advice, both about the development and any other possibilities. 'It would be potentially very damaging to the Company if, once the Development was proceeded with at Robroyston, the press were to misconstrue Mr Dempsey's involvement in the matter in the light of the Board's reluctance to pursue other projects and take proper professional advice. This could, at best, make the Board appear foolish and, at worst, give rise to suspicion of impropriety.'

They went on: 'If it is the case that Mr Dempsey, through SL Homes Ltd, is actively involved in the development of land at Robroyston by Nardlaw, he might have such a severe conflict of interest as to render it almost impossible for him to be seen to be acting in the best interests of Celtic.'

I was also reminded that shareholders are entitled to assume that anyone being put forward to them as a candidate for election as a director has the full blessing of the company's Board. If the Board, having fully discussed the matter, decided to continue their support for Dempsey's election as a director, two options were open to me. The first was to resign as a director. Or I could remain as a director of the company with some chance, in that position, of protecting the interests of the shareholders. That advice was accompanied by a fee note, which was, of course, my personal responsiblity.

My solicitor's advice gave me no choice. It was my duty as a director to inform the Board about the matter. But first, on the Tuesday before, I told Chris, the Club Secretary, what I had been told by Nick Farrell. Chris raised the matter with McGinn as chairman, and indicated that he should raise it with the Board at its meeting on the Thursday.

McGinn presented the facts about Nardlaw to the Board and asked Dempsey for an explanation.

Dempsey reminded the Board that he had earlier told us that he had tried to buy land at Robroyston for the Club but that, if he did, Jaymarke would call the proposed joint venture off. He pointed out that he was involved in other deals with Jaymarke in England. Land that he had purchased jointly with Jaymarke had cost SL Homes £325,000, and this had saved Celtic money.

Chris wanted to know why Dempsey had not informed the Board about the existence of Nardlaw, particularly as it had actually bought land adjacent to the proposed stadium development site.

But this was not what exercised the rest of the directors. They were more concerned about my role in raising the matter. I pointed out that it had not been an easy decision for me until I had received clear legal advice in writing that I was obliged to raise the matter with the Board.

Dempsey claimed that being involved with Celtic only cost him money and that Chris and I had thrown one obstacle after another in the path of the Robroyston proposals, without having any constructive ideas of our own. Chris made it clear that he thought that Dempsey was the one who rubbished every other option as it was proposed. He also reminded the Board that they had now whole-heartedly embraced the idea of sharing the national stadium, which had been my proposal.

The Board meeting was then interrupted so that we could

meet, as planned, Wilson and Shaw of Jaymarke. They confirmed Dempsey's explanation of Nardlaw:

'Shaw stated that Jaymarke had had its eyes on the site after buying Robroyston. They thought they had a deal struck with Caltrust. P & O said Celtic were "on to" this piece of ground. Jaymarke thought that Celtic were "doing" them by spinning them along on the main site while buying up the small site for a stadium.

'Jaymarke insisted that Mr Dempsey withdraw and if Jaymarke were successful they would come back and talk. The site cost more than they expected. It was logical to go back to Mr Dempsey and say "where do we stand"? They then went in to a deal with Mr Dempsey to buy the land. From their point of view it did not matter who they were dealing with.'

After a detailed discussion about the proposed agreement with Jaymarke, the Celtic Board meeting resumed. I was pressed for the source of all of the information about Nardlaw. I refused to go further than emphasise that it came not from some disgruntled third party, but from a shareholder who had a legitimate interest in the company's affairs. But I had told Nick Farrell that I would be raising the matter. He agreed that I should, and arranged to tell his father after the Board meeting. I have no idea what the reaction was.

The Board had to decide whether to accept Dempsey's explanations about Nardlaw's existence. We all eventually did, but Chris, in going along with this, asked Dempsey to accept that he was wrong in not bringing the existence of Nardlaw to the attention of the directors. Dempsey refused to accept this, and, in a heated exchange, 'went on to voice the depth of his contempt for Mr White'.

Farrell then proposed the removal of the independent solicitors that he had chosen, on the basis that they weren't needed any more. Chris moved to keep them because he felt that, 'with the conflicts of interest and personality existing on the Board it would be in the Club's interest to maintain independent legal advisers'.

I supported Chris, but we lost the vote five-two. I refused to accept that there was no need for independent advice because 'the interests of the different parties were not sufficiently clarified'.

Chris then asked permission to discuss funding for Robroyston with the bank, but was told this would be 'premature'. Chris also felt that the discovery of the existence of Nardlaw and the question of conflict of interest needed to be put to the shareholders at the imminent Annual General Meeting. Farrell told him to consult his own legal advisers privately.

During the earlier meeting with Jaymarke, Shaw again refused point blank to modify the planning trigger for the transfer to Celtic of the stadium site, because 'it would be relatively easy for Celtic to guide the project towards getting only stadium planning, if things were proving difficult'. This confirmed my feeling that Celtic was being used as a vehicle to help Jaymarke, not the other way round.

Farrell stated that 'his partners had pointed out that the wording chosen was in everyone's interests', while I argued that, with planning permission for the stadium alone, we would have no planning gain and therefore be unable to build it.

One of my concerns had been the short timescale demanded by the agreements for a decision. While Jaymarke now were prepared to extend the option period by some three months to January 1991, it still didn't seem sufficient time to assess the project and ascertain whether we could fund it. They were really willing to concede very little. Our choice now was 'take it or leave it'.

Chris and I digested the situation for a couple more days. Our conclusion was that Robroyston had to be halted, but that we were never going to convince any of the other directors how dangerous it really was. So we had to oppose Dempsey's confirmation as a director, which was, along with my own confirmation, an item on the agenda of the forthcoming AGM. I was very uneasy about doing it because I knew the trouble it would cause. It would not be over and done with on the night, it would be a festering irritation for years. Uncharacteristically, I decided to duck the issue.

On Friday 26 October 1990, the day of the AGM, Chris called me to a meeting in Francis McCrossin's office at two o'clock. Francis and Ronald Gordon, Chris's solicitor, were in attendance. I expected a further discusssion about Dempsey and had all the arguments prepared to urge caution. But Chris didn't give me a chance to say anything. Rather, almost before I sat down, he took the initiative and simply said: 'I will be opposing Brian Dempsey's confirmation this evening, and I expect you to give me your full support.' With a sinking feeling, I agreed, because it was the right thing to do. I warned Chris there could be years of strife. 'It doesn't matter,' he said. 'It has to be done for Celtic.'

We had taken the precaution of ensuring that all the proxies that we needed to win the votes at the AGM were duly lodged. I had to phone around those supportive shareholders who always came in person, to brief them on the situation and secure their votes. I made the calls from my office with a heavy heart, but I did not encounter a single dissenter.

The meeting was scheduled for seven o'clock and the Board had arranged to convene at six for a meal in the Walfrid Restaurant, to review boring pre-AGM matters – for example, who was to move and second each item on agenda. Chris and I had disagreed over whether anything should be said in advance of the AGM. Chris simply wanted to do and say nothing until the item on the agenda was called, then vote against Dempsey. I insisted that we told Dempsey to his face and the rest of the Board before the meeting. The last thing I wanted was a meal, so I didn't rush to turn up at six. (Tom Grant later said that had made him suspicious.) At half-past I joined the rest of the Board in the restaurant. I ate nothing, ordered a lime and soda, and watched Chris eat his way through a full three-course meal, ending with black forest gateau and cream. Chris might dither for a long time over the most trivial of decisions – but once he had made up his mind, even over an issue as momentous as this one, he never worried about it afterwards.

We went into the chairman's office, worked quickly through the agenda, then got to the item for the confirmation of the co-opted directors. I said: 'I am not going to be supporting Brian Dempsey's ratification.' There was consternation and outrage, particularly from Grant, Farrell and McGinn. Farrell asked Chris what he was going to do. Chris was quite pedantic about it. 'I was not going to volunteer anything just now,' he started, 'but if you are asking me a direct question I can tell you that I will be voting against Brian's confirmation.' Then various people said they would oppose my confirmation, but I had the comfort of knowing that we had the votes in the bag. In the event, Grant voted for me because he said he'd supported both of us when we were being co-opted.

Dempsey turned to the others and asked: 'What do you want

51

me to do?' Afterwards, he claimed he'd said: 'Put me on tonight and I'll resign within three months', so that he wouldn't be publicly embarrassed. Different versions of this are given by Low and Caldwell. In Caldwell's book, Dempsey claims that he 'offered to write a quick letter of resignation which they could announce after the final'. Low claims Dempsey offered to 'wait until the season was over to avoid a bublic [sic] row'. I don't remember his saying anything like that − even if he had, once you're on the Board you're on for three years and nobody can do anything about it without calling an EGM − and we would soon know the trouble they can cause. I didn't trust him or the others to honour any verbal commitment, so I wouldn't have gone along with it anyway.

Silently, we went upstairs to the Jock Stein Lounge for the AGM. I sat between Grant and Billy McNeill. We came to the controversial item on the agenda. McGinn tried to put Dempsey's name forward before mine, reversing the agenda order, possibly thinking that exposing our move might provoke a backlash against me when my turn came. Ronald Gordon (proxy for Chris's mother) insisted on the order as written on the circulated agenda, with the vote on my confirmation being taken first. McGinn, as chairman, could have ridden roughshod over this intervention but he just caved in. If the votes had been taken the other way round, I can't see that the result would have been any different.

I won my vote. Chris moved his opposition to Dempsey firmly and eloquently, citing fundamental differences over policy. Farrell made one of his now-famous impassioned and rambling speeches on Dempsey's behalf. Smaller shareholders sat shocked, asked for explanations. Chris refused to elaborate. Dempsey put forward his case, to the effect that he wanted only to see Celtic prosper and that Robroyston offered the best way out of the stadium dilemma. Dempsey won the vote on a show of hands by seventeen votes to thirteen. The poll vote was taken, at Chris's request, counting not shareholders but numbers of shares and Dempsey was no longer a director of Celtic Football Club by a majority of 733 to 472.

Traditionally, the manager attends the AGM to give a report on the playing side. Early on in the meeting when it became obvious that this was not going to be the usual annual formality that Celtic shareholders had become used to, I said quietly to

McNeill: 'You don't want involved in this, you'd be better leaving.' He did. But before he left to go back to Seamill and the team, with Sunday's Skol Cup Final against Rangers in mind, I asked what effect all this would have on the team. He said: 'It won't have any effect at all – the players don't even know the names of the directors!' In the event, Dziekanowski missed an open goal in extra time before Gough scored the winner. It was the first of many unhelpful results on the park in the following years. In fact, it is difficult to recall a single helpful outcome of a game at any subsequent critical point in the Celtic takeover saga. Only in the last few months of the drama was there any suggestion that some players were conspiring with the rebels, so I am certainly not arguing that the lack of success on the park was deliberate. But it was certainly against the law of averages. Maybe that's what you deserve when you have a below average team.

The removal of Dempsey was the central event in the whole of the struggle for Celtic's soul. If he had survived, the Club would have signed the Robroyston papers and been committed to a project that I believe would have placed impossible capital demands on it. Then there would have been a call for additional equity to be injected; and the family shareholders would have been supplanted as the owners of Celtic. That's how I saw the game plan at the time. Nothing else made sense. The agreements with Jaymarke were ones that no director should have accepted. The development wasn't funded and it hadn't the remotest chance of satisfying the planners. So why was it being pushed so strongly? Because, under it, the obligations on Celtic were such that to fulfil even the most immediate of them would have required the existing shareholders to relinquish control.

But it was an irresponsible way to try to achieve it. Even someone who genuinely thought that the Club could not make any progress without such a change should have been deterred by the unrealistic risks involved in this way of attempting to secure it.

Chapter Five

And study of revenge, immortal hate,
And courage, never to submit or yield . . . .

Paradise Lost, 1.105

I didn't handle the aftermath of Dempsey's removal at all well. What was needed, I now see, was ruthless and decisive action to establish firm control and a clear way forward. What we allowed to develop in the critical first weeks was a power and policy vacuum.

The first task should have been to explain clearly to the public exactly why Dempsey had been removed. But, I felt severely inhibited in trying to do this. For one thing, I had no intention at all of trying to take over the running of the Club myself. I certainly didn't want to be chief executive, partly because I was enjoying running my own successful business and partly because I didn't want to usurp Kevin's position. Rightly or wrongly, Bob Kelly had chosen him to carry on the family tradition.

Again, I don't think that Chris would have wanted me to promote myself. I was there to help him implement his plans for change. So I persuaded him to take the lead role that weekend. He was very happy with the private aspects of this (for example, he laid down the law to McGinn, first thing that Saturday morning). But, he was extremely reluctant to act in public, which was an equally important side of things. And he had had no training or experience in dealing with the media. In particular, he had no affinity with the live radio performance which has become an increasingly important part of football journalism. Persuading him to phone in a stumbling statement live on Radio Clyde that aftenoon, and for him to put the phone down before he could be asked any questions, was a big mistake. Quite frankly, I bungled the media relations that Saturday.

But I really didn't know what to say that would be accepted as an adequate explanation. What line could I take which wouldn't seem openly critical of Grant, Kevin or McGinn, all of whom we were hoping to continue to work with, for we had no plans to try to throw anyone else off the Board. Neither did I want to sling mud. I wanted Celtic to escape from the mess and into a better, more secure future. On the stadium front, I had nothing specific to offer because all the running had been made by Dempsey with his Robroyston scheme and none of the other options that the Board had casually considered had been developed. The Robroyston scheme was perceived by the fans as being the only one with any hope of achieving what we all wanted to achieve.

Chris did go on record that weekend saying that 'various stadium options had been looked at over the last six months, but no one had worked out the actual funding'. He also announced that the aim now was to 'build up the Club's income and improve profitablity to see what could be afforded in the way of developments'. And he announced 'immediate steps to appoint a chief executive to strengthen the commercial side of the Club'. He made the simple point that we had been considering embarking on a multi-million pound investment with a weak trading position that could not support the increased debt involved. A chief executive would determine how much the trading could be improved and therefore what level of debt could prudently be sustained.

Dempsey's removal was greeted with fury by Scotland's sporting Press, who understandably read it solely as a refusal by the traditional families to tolerate any interference in the way in which they ran the Club. The story developed of a personal difference between myself and Dempsey. Later, the rumour circulated that Dempsey had been trying to change things too fast. Farrell told me that he had told Dempsey that his mistake was in not getting close enough to Chris and me.

The truth was simpler. Robroyston was a half-baked, unfunded scheme that, in my opinion, would have proved ruinous for Celtic. Another way had to be found, and Dempsey was not the person to look for that solution.

A number of journalists have since told me that to tell the detailed story of the reasons for Dempsey's removal right away would have ended the matter. Given the Press's subsequent subservience to the rebels, I doubt it. And anyway, there were good reasons for keeping quiet. The main reason was to protect Kevin – and, to a certain extent, Grant – from ridicule. They had vigorously promoted Dempsey and Robroyston. Exposing the scheme for what it was would have shown them up as naïve at best. It would also have made it even less likely that they would go along with anything which Chris and I proposed. The situation on the Board was a very difficult one for us. We were outnumbered four-to-two. So we needed to mend fences, not humiliate individuals in public.

The day after the AGM, a Saturday, Chris called McGinn to his house. McGinn may have realised that at last Chris had decided to exercise the enormous power that he had as the biggest shareholder. He might have been prepared to resign, but Chris didn't ask him to. Rather, he reminded him that it was Desmond who had put McGinn on the Board, and that he (McGinn) had failed in his promise to be loyal to Chris. He was told he could stay on if he toed the line – which he did until the crucial last day.

Media reaction, in the absence of any clear explanation of events was understandably negative and – given their adulation of Dempsey as saviour of the Club – angry. It was important, though, to demonstrate clearly to the outside world that the new situation had come about because the largest shareholder, Chris White, had made his judgment on Dempsey. Chris was therefore the unequivocal new power base at Celtic Park – that was why he had to make himself freely available for interview by the media, as the man in charge of the Club. He was paraded around the city . . . Scottish Television, BBC Television, Radio Scotland and Radio Clyde. For a few weeks, anyway.

Chris didn't relish the role of leader, and didn't enjoy the media experience; he didn't want to take on the chairmanship, and wasn't suited to it. He was a man of great strength of mind, but he was not a public personality. We needed to search elsewhere for someone with this curious 20th-century characteristic.

The atmosphere within the Board in the wake of the AGM was one of tremendous hostility towards Chris and me, accompanied by a kind of collective humiliation and embarrassment that they had proved to be so neutered in the face of legitimate shareholder power. The weeks which followed the AGM were laced with deepest gloom and a sense of helplessness. But a letter to the *Glasgow Herald* (as it was then called) confirmed that the stance taken by Chris and me might not have been completely wrong.

October 29.

Sir – When viewed within the context of the continuing financial evolution of Scottish football structures the events at the Celtic Football Club annual general meeting (October 27) should not have been unexpected by those who are familiar with the financial requirements of premier-league football teams in the 1990s and beyond.

Furthermore, on the basis of what public information there is, I believe the non-ratification of Mr Dempsey is correct.

Contrary to the public sayings of the Scottish Football League, Scottish football is massively undercapitalised and none more so than Celtic. They will have problems raising the level of funding required for impending UEFA regulations and implementations of the Taylor Report.

When Celtic's financial situation is observed from this standpoint it is utter folly for responsible directors and shareholders to attempt to bind the club to such a level of capital commitment as the Robroyston proposal would do without first securing the means of finance and method of repayment.

The importance of this issue has recently been amplified by the Football Trust's decision to cap assistance to premier-league club refurbishment at £2m per club.

To ignore this fundamental tenet is to expose 100 years of tradition and excellence to the excesses of the capitalist system as suffered by Hibs supporters recently.

Mr White and Dr Kelly are to be congratulated for their foresight and the efficient manner in which they sought to preserve all that Celtic Football Club stands for.

David Low

David Low has been described as 'a financial mercenary', prepared to go and fight the fiercest of financial battles. He had been a client of mine in the takeover battle for the cash-rich remains of Bremners, the former Glasgow department store – a battle which ended, with complete success from our side's point of view, when it was transformed into an investment trust.

He convinced me that he was clever and knowledgeable about the intricacies of corporate finance and company law. He knew a trick or two. But Low's taste for high-profile financial manoeuvrings contrasted badly with an untelegenic

57

persona which made him unsuitable for media appearances. He became fascinated by the football scene and made several attempts to 'help' Scottish clubs. He also hired me to promote the idea of Dublin City joining the Scottish League, for which crazy story I got him a front page splash in the *Daily Record*. So Low was able to put himself about as a 'football analyst', which suited various journalists seeking a spurious 'independent' view. When he 'changed sides' and started courting Dempsey, he was briefly paraded as a man in the know. But following a mauling on Radio Clyde from Terry Cassidy, Low was hardly ever seen or heard again on the airwaves.

He was, however, working away in the background and soon teamed up with Dempsey. During our business dealings Low and I always had time to chat about Celtic. He was very anxious to get involved and asked me about the chances of his buying shares. I couldn't help him there as Board policy was quite clear: shares were to be transferred only within family groups, and no precedents were to be set. This refusal to help must have irritated him. He says in his book that from then on he 'began to view [Michael Kelly] in a different light'. So he became another of the many people we used to see come and go at Celtic Park – people, envious of the private club they saw it to be, who had their offers of involvement firmly rejected and who then became critics and detractors crushing the grapes of wrath.

Low linked up with the man who had taken a business decision so personally. Dempsey was seen by him as being able to 'have a thorough-going four-lettered row with colleagues . . . and, once a decision had been reached, carry on as before, no grudges or resentments nursed'. But this magnanimity was a one-way street. Dempsey's reaction was not so generous when he was on the receiving end, and I believe the bitterness that he felt after his removal from the Board fuelled a campaign against the Club that was to reduce it to its lowest ebb.

These two teamed up to seize control of Celtic or to bring it down in the process. Low travelled widely at home and abroad with irrevocable bank drafts, buying up share proxies on behalf of the rebel consortium. He was well remunerated for his efforts. Though he is coy about revealing this part of the strategy, he was paid over £16,000 by the rebel consortium in February 1994; and of course after the takeover he was rewarded with the ultimate badge of acceptability, a seat in the Box. Maybe one

58

day he will get what used to be Farrell's job under my uncle's rule – handing out tickets to other guests.

Nevertheless, Low's letter immediately after the AGM was about the only support we got in the sea of emotional claptrap echoing around the sports pages. The only other supporter was one Gerry McSherry, who conducted a lonely counter-campaign over the next four years. In public-relations terms, it was therefore important to fill the vacuum appearing in the perception of Celtic's progress on the stadium issue.

As it happened, the Glasgow-based consulting engineers Sir William Halcrow & Partners Scotland Ltd, who were by then my clients, had a year earlier submitted a plan for redeveloping Celtic Park to Tom Grant. It provided for a 52,000-seat stadium, with a new Jungle stand cantilevered out over Janefield Street, and the pitch being moved slightly south and east to allow additional seating, at the same time dispensing with the now-unused running track which surrounds the existing pitch.

In order to demonstrate that there was life beyond Robroyston, I decided to publish details of this plan for the re-development of Celtic Park. A cost of £30 million had been put on the scheme. Later, other engineers and architects put forward a variety of such schemes, with price tags ranging from £10 million to £35 million. The last of these proposals was that of Fergus McCann. His scheme, announced a couple of weeks after he came to power, came with the obligatory artist's impression, and – sticking to the equally rigid convention – no detailed funding package. It was just another variation of what we knew at the time: it was physically possible, but a tight squeeze, to rebuild Celtic Park. But no matter what the scheme, the financing of it never stacked up.

We presented the Halcrow scheme to the members of the executive club in early November, but there was great scepticism about it: where was the money to come from? It was clear that most of them thought that the only solution to the stadium problem was to start afresh on a new site, allied to a commercial development such as housing. That, indeed, had become the conventional wisdom, but everyone seemed to assume that Robroyston was the only new site where such a new stadium could be built.

But we couldn't put the events of the AGM behind us. A conversation between Farrell and Chris, in which Chris had asked

59

Farrell '. . . in view of your pro-Dempsey views, are you going to resign?' was leaked just to keep the controversy going.

Jim Craig, the player who gave away the penalty in Lisbon, was given the freedom of the Catholic newspaper *Flourish* to ponder: 'I would like to know what the crime Brian Dempsey committed which necessitated him [sic] leaving the Board.'

We had annoyed and puzzled the Press. For example, the *Sunday Mail* of 9 December 1990: 'It has never been fully understood, nor do I think it has been adequately explained, why Dempsey had to leave.' And that sentiment remained until the takeover by McCann four years later.

Jim Traynor of the *Glasgow Herald*, a man with his own morose and suspicious approach, correctly identified the bruised egos that we never succeeded in healing. On 26 November 1990, he wrote:

> [Dempsey] could return to haunt them all. Just as there were ways of removing him, there are methods of bringing him back. Significantly, the hurt of those who felt insulted by the manner in which Dempsey was removed should not be underestimated. They will fight back because the future of a club, which like Rangers is interwoven in Glasgow's heritage, is at stake and traumatic times lie ahead.
>
> 'Celtic's directors are so deeply divided the rift might never be bridged and amid the simmering resentment, minds continue to plot. Directors have assumed stances and a battle of politics, perhaps even of mathematics as shareholdings and proxies are brought forward, will be fought.
>
> 'White and Kelly may have made the mistake of not bolting the boardroom door when they closed it on Dempsey. They should have left him no way back.

We were outnumbered on the Board by four-to-two, though McGinn's compliance might produce a three-three vote on most issues. Chris and I needed a period of time to win them over. Or we needed to shift the voting balance within the Board. But how? And how long would it take?

We agreed on a strategy to achieve better harmony – the appointment of a chief executive. Such an appointment would serve to take away executive power from the Board, and to control the maverick tendencies of Grant and McGinn who, with Chris, had considerable executive discretion within the Club. The Board could step back from the endlessly divisive meetings. Naturally enough, the proposal for a chief executive was itself greeted with great suspicion by the others. They clearly expected me to be the likely person to be appointed, and this prospect was not pleasing to them.

McGinn, who had been executive chairman and general manager since 1986, would effectively be replaced. Despite the internal bickerings, there was general agreement among all members of the Board about McGinn's capabilities, and we agreed in principle to advertise for a chief executive. When it was revealed that all the candidates to be interviewed would be from outside the Club, the members of the Board – no doubt relieved I was not among them – agreed to go ahead.

The chief executive's job description was drawn up by Douglas Kinnaird, the personable head of the PA Consulting Group in Glasgow, in November 1990. The interviews were to be held in December. One hundred and thirty people replied to the advertisement, including Dominic Keane. Kinnaird drew up his own short-leet of those to be head-hunted, recommending five candidates. Two of them, already at chief executive level with other companies, declined to accept the invitation to interview. Two others joined Terry Cassidy on the list for a job offering a £95,000 package of remuneration.

Kinnaird had prepared a short dossier on each candidate. It described each man's career, commenting on and assessing various aspects based on preliminary investigations and assessments made by the agency. Of the three candidates, Cassidy's 'Competency Profile' – and the accompanying personal assessment report – was unquestionably the best. It began: 'Cassidy is in the top class of business managers. He makes an immediate and lasting impression of toughness, but he is also good fun, pleasant company and completely down-to-earth. He is a born salesman, who does not realise just how good he is.'

It noted Cassidy had played for Nottingham Forest, but within six months a serious injury ended his career. As a businessman, he had established such a good reputation that he was appointed managing director of George Outram & Co, a SUITS subsidiary, part of the Lonhro Group. In his five years in the job, he turned a loss-making situation around in dramatic fashion by investing heavily in new high-tech equipment, despite opposition from powerful trade unions.

According to the profile, Cassidy said he liked 'doing things other people cannot do' and 'could do the Celtic job standing on [his] head'. It concluded that Cassidy was 'an absolutely ideal candidate, he is a natural man-manager, whom everyone would enjoy working with and for . . . He is not scared of any tasks; he has very strong views and is not scared to voice them.' It added an important observation which Cassidy had made, that he considered the job to be a general manager's position rather than that of a chief executive, because a seat on the Board was not being offered.

In the margins of my copy of the PA Consulting Group briefing document, I made notes as the interview progressed:

> Only one of the short-leet who has real chief executive experience . . . Broad, not narrow. Would allow other managers to breathe, especially McNeill, but also TG, CW, etc . . . For this job at this time, the only choice . . . Age, experience are important in the situation we are in . . . Postholder would be on trial with Press and fans. Cassidy would be accepted as a brilliant choice . . . Will he come? . . . Understands enormity of job, feeling in Glasgow, demands of Press and fans . . . Geordie background gives him football insight . . . actually did play! . . . Stature . . .

And then, significantly: 'If McNeill is to go, who would you want to handle the aftermath?' That was a question I was not able to answer with conviction in my marginal notes, but everything else stacked up in Cassidy's favour.

Nevertheless, Grant and Farrell both opposed Cassidy's appointment, going for a person better qualified to be a sales director, having run Blackpool Tower Circus. You can imagine the public impact that would have had!

Cassidy started work immediately after the New Year break. The first problem he had to deal with was the two executive directors who reported to him, although he himself was not a director. In retrospect he should have been, but there was no chance of that Board agreeing to it. Chris didn't want him on the Board either. It was better to try him out first, he said, and let him move gradually to a place on the Board. So Cassidy was in attendance at Board meetings for most of the time, but left when shareholders' interests were discussed. All credit should, however, go to Grant: he accepted Cassidy as his superior in management terms and worked faithfully for him. Chris, however, had a worse experience. He is a terrible timekeeper, though he always worked long and hard. But he is often not at his desk by nine o'clock. For this, he was continually pulled up by Cassidy – a silly act, really, which may have made a point at the expense of common sense.

Cassidy's objectives, set by the Board, were to solve the stadium issue and to restore profitability to the Club. In his first few weeks, we had a feeling of exhilaration that at last we had someone working on these overwhelmingly complex twin problems who had the track record to make something happen. For a short time, we were able to relax.

But he was entering a totally hostile external environment. Since the Skol Cup Final defeat results had not been good, and at New Year Rangers beat us for the third time that season. This provoked the predictable crisis headlines in all the papers. The fans had become increasingly unhappy with McNeill's performance, and after a three-one defeat at Tannadice in December they had demonstrated against him. But the Press weren't for that – they laid the blame firmly on the Board. While the manager's mistakes were acknowledged and the players criticised, it was the directors the tabloids – and the 'qualities' as well – were gunning for. Thus a catalogue of expensive signings estimated at £4.4 million was 'a spending spree which ended in disaster' and not a genuine attempt by the directors to give the manager the money he needed to build a team.

So, despite the fact that it was money badly spent rather than no money available that was the problem, the conclusion of the *Daily Record* was 'Bring Back Dempsey' – not, as the facts suggested, 'Sack the Manager'. They therefore set their campaign theme for the next four years, and no facts were going to interfere with that.

The performance of the team, combined with the disgust generated by Dempsey's removal, saw the emergence for the first time of another sinister development. Sponsors, box-holders, executive club members and advertisers were said to be considering withdrawing their financial support. One sponsor, Gerry

Gallagher, described naturally as a 'tycoon' although he was only proposing to spend £13,000 for the rest of the season, was the first to be specified. This tactic had been mooted in the immediate aftermath of the AGM and had been given strong support by the Press, but this was its first concrete manifestation.

In the *Daily Express* on 11 December 1990, bemoaning the loss of the person he continued to champion, Dempsey, Gerry McNee announced his agenda: 'White and Kelly axed a man with commitment and guts, who was prepared to go out on a limb and take the decisions necessary to put the Club back on top.' He went on: 'Only one factor will bring about the necessary change now – the Celtic supporters. They have been too loyal and too understanding for too long. Celtic directors cannot maintain power without the fans' financial support. Unless they mobilise, organise and dictate who runs the Club, those who are left will probably be supporting a team with second-class ambitions.'

This was the beginning of an orchestrated campaign to bring down the Board.

Dempsey distanced himself publicly from the move. Quoted in the *Sun* on 9 January 1991, he rapped(!): 'Removing financial support from the club would not be in anybody's interest.' On 24 May 1991 Dempsey announced that he was withdrawing from his Skybox. The papers had put his spending with Celtic at £350,000, but Cassidy asked my firm to announce that the figure for season 1990-91 had been £116,654. This was largely ignored.

Cassidy fell out with the Press immediately and irretrievably. It was the shortest honeymoon since Bluebeard's second marriage. He gave an interview to *Scotland on Sunday* on 6 January 1991 in which he was bold enough to criticise sports writers in his abrasive way. 'Some of them,' he said, 'are just anti-Celtic. But the same buggers would be queuing up to get on the gravy-train if Celtic were back riding high. And wouldn't they be hurt if they weren't allowed on board.'

The paper's diarist instantly picked up the truth and implications of this statement. The following week he wrote: 'Cassidy has vowed that certain writers will be excluded from the Parkhead gravy-train. Expect more "Celtic in crisis" exclusives soon, accompanied by hymns of praise for go-getting Rangers, the club which holds a champagne reception at the drop of a football hack's pencil.'

Years later, the *Sunday Mail* observed that Dempsey was not the kind of person to make such a mistake. Commenting on the events of Takeover Friday, it noted that the Press had been fed and watered on Brian Dempsey's instructions. Instead of leaving Celtic to foot the cost he had 'gladly' picked up a bill for £302 himself, they claimed. Why not, if he had ordered it, one asks? But the point was to contrast this gesture with the presumed behaviour of the deposed regime who would not pay for anything. 'There will, it announced pompously, be no more freeloaders at Celtic Park.' Who then drank the £302 worth of hospitality?

Cassidy's *Scotland on Sunday* article earned him an editorial in the *Daily Record*: 'Cassidy's bully-boy tactics will assuredly rebound.' And Jim Traynor in the *Herald* was depressed at Cassidy's start because 'only a few days into his job he had upset Brian Dempsey'.

This was the beginning of the ludicrous Press coverage. The *Sunday Mail* carried the news that 'Chris White last night gave the green light for Brian Dempsey to rejoin the Parkhead Board'! That was David Leggat's interpretation of a statement by Chris that 'Mr Cassidy has my full backing in anything he intends to do'. As every business journalist knows, one of the things an employee cannot do is to co-opt new directors.

Even the *Observer* preferred the fanciful to the factual. This was its version of the AGM of which you now know the facts: 'A meal had been arranged before the last annual general meeting. It turned out to be the last supper. As the directors rose from the table, Kelly told Dempsey he would be voted off the board. The victim of a ruthless coup, he was therefore unable to put his tempting ideas to the share-holders.'

So, going into 1991 the battle lines were clearly drawn. On the one hand, there was Chris and me. On the other, the rest of the directors, who were disaffected to a greater or lesser degree, Dempsey and his business supporters, a proportion of the ordinary fans and the Press. For us to succeed we needed the chief executive to produce an improved commercial position and the manager to deliver a degree of success on the field.

Certainly, Cassidy made progress on the commercial front. Through Peter Lawell, the financial controller, budgets and management accounts were produced for the first time. Going into the 1991-92 season, sales of season tickets were up. Mobile shops were introduced later that year, and Peoples were announced as new shirt sponsors. The greatest coup of all was the new kit sponsorship deal with Umbro. This was an eight-year, £11 million deal. So good was it, the best at its time in all of British football, that we produced all the financial details so that the Press would believe it.

But still there was criticism. McNee, who had got the name of the new sponsors absolutely wrong, had to find fault somewhere: 'Their timing, the morning after a Euro-exit, has to go down as yet another PR disaster.' It wasn't the long-term deal that was important, it was the last result!

Cassidy even introduced modern electronic scoreboards on which messages and advertising could be displayed. On a quiet afternoon, John Thomson, Michael Kelly Associates' resident football comedian, produced the following list of messages which could be flashed up as appropriate during games.

Some of them still make me smile.

KICK OFF
  Come On Ra' Tic
  Here we go, Here we go, Here we go
  Let's kick ass, Celts
  Give us four, Celts

HOME GOAL
  That was worth waiting for, Tony
  How about another one before Liam subs you, Charlie
  Great vision, Tommy
  Give us another one

HOME PENALTY
  At long last, ref!
  OFF, OFF, OFF
  Good Luck [Whoever]
  To his right, Charlie
  That fooled you, Andy

GUEST PENALTY
   He never touched him
   I don't believe it
   Never!
   Come on, Packie
   He's missed it
   Great save, Packie

GUEST GOAL
   Oh No!
   Come on Celts, let's get it back
   We don't believe it
   Come on, linesman, we could see it was offside from here

KICKING THE BALL INTO TOUCH FOR AN INJURED PLAYER
   What a sportsman!

NOT KICKING THE BALL INTO TOUCH FOR AN INJURED PLAYER
   You Rotter!
   You Hun! [special occasions]

THE FINAL WHISTLE
   Didn't we do well?
   It can only get better
   Thanks Team
   Thanks To A Great Support
   See you in a Fortnight

The amazing thing is that the Press got no word of this at all – otherwise it would have been another PR disaster. It wouldn't have been played as a joke.

Chapter Six

... To sit in darkness here
Hatching vain empires ...

Paradise Lost, 1.377

Billy McNeill was always very relaxed when giving his reports
of on-the-park happenings to Board meetings. He was adept
at handling the disparate group of directors, and invariably
succeeded in getting his own way – one measure of a good
manager. A trivial example, but one which makes the point,
was in the discussion of bonuses for the 1991 Tennent Sixes
competition. The bonus structure for the ordinary games was
decided at the beginning of the season, but the Sixes were not
covered by this. Billy raised the question, in early January, seeking
bonuses for winning the section, the semi and the final, in line
with payments to the Club. I argued that, given the pathetic
performance of the team, they should be asked to go out and
win the tournament as a way of apology to the fans. As Rangers
weren't competing, who was there to beat? I got very little support
and in the discussion formed the clear impression that it had been
cut and dried between the manager and the chairman long before
the meeting. Celtic didn't win the Sixes that year. In fact, we never
even qualified from our section.

I recall one of the earliest Board meetings I ever attended, when
McNeill unwittingly strayed into dangerous territory – the matter
of players' 'backgrounds'. Reporting to the Board about various
players who were interesting him as potential transfer targets he
told us of his interest in David Winnie, then playing for St Mirren.
Suddenly he remarked in an aside to Grant: 'And he's a Tim!' This
would have passed without comment if I hadn't interrupted to ask,
'Wait a minute, Billy, what do you mean? What possible relevance
has religion got to do with this?'

With hindsight, I must have sounded rather pedantic but
I persisted with my querulousness, to be asked in turn by

the manager: 'Who said anything about religion?' There then followed a tortuous discussion about the meaning and derivation of 'Tim'. Linguist McGinn (remember 'lunAtic'?) insisted it was an abbreviation of 'Tim Malloy', rhyming slang for 'Bhoy', an Irishman. 'Oh, then Winnie's Irish?' I said. Luckily, it wasn't Jack Charlton that I was asking or the answer almost certainly would have been 'yes'!

McNeill then clarified his meaning. He felt, he said, that players who had been Celtic supporters as boys normally showed a greater appetite and enthusiasm for the Club as players. I thought that this was dangerous rubbish. I know that it is an assumption that a lot of Celtic people share – that West of Scotland players of a Catholic or Irish background will try that bit harder for Celtic. To me that is a cultural myth, nothing more, and I just do not believe it. So disgusted am I by the suggestion, which attacks one of the fundamental principles on which the Club is run, that I refuse to search to produce examples of non-Catholics who have played their hearts out for the Club.

But it is a widespread view. I remember, long before I was on the Board, being approached by a fan as I came out of the main door after a bad home defeat. 'The balance of the team is wrong,' he said. 'It can't be more than seven-four.' It didn't sound like any formation I had heard of, so I asked him what he was talking about. 'We can't have any more than four of they other people,' he said. Despite the vehemence of my reaction, I couldn't shake his conviction. Indeed, at the end of a heated conversation, he was beginning to doubt my credentials, which is exactly how bigots think. I could not have selected the 'other people' from that team with any certainty – and, thank God, I still couldn't with the present squad. Who cares? As far as I am concerned, players play first and foremost for their own personal pride. There are then the questions of the individual's personality, his morale on the particular day and the motivational power of the manager. It's as simple and as complex as that.

On this question of Celtic's relationship to the Catholic Church, Chris had an amusing conversation with the businessman organising the Billy Graham visit to Scotland in 1991. The organising committee wanted to hold the Glasgow rally at Celtic Park, and the chairman phoned Chris to sound him out on the idea. 'And I've cleared it with the Archbishop,' he concluded. Chris, whose religious observance is sporadic, was horrified that anyone would think that the Archbishop's opinion on this would hold any sway at all. But I don't think he could convince the caller.

At the beginning of January 1991, as Cassidy settled into his new office (which McGinn graciously had given up as the chairman's suite), McNeill's job was on the line. We hadn't won a trophy for eighteen months, we'd lost the Skol Cup Final and the Ne'erday Old Firm match two-nothing. This was bracketed by a draw at home against Hearts and a draw at Easter Road against bottom-placed Hibs. This extended to six our run of games without a win during the most crucial period of any League season. Now fifteen points behind the leaders, Rangers, it wasn't being disloyal to recognise that we were not going to win the League. Even qualification for Europe was going to be a struggle as we were nine points behind the third place that was the minimum we needed.

The Board had last discussed the management of the team in the previous (1990-91) close season, just days after the painful Cup Final defeat by Aberdeen. The manager assessed the position and put forward his plans for strengthening the team. The Board decided to endorse his proposals and gave him the financial backing to implement them. After specifying the players whom he wanted and what he thought that he would have to pay for them, he was given a free hand to go and get them. In the event, he spent £2 million on Martin Hayes, Charlie Nicholas and John Collins. But he was also given a clear warning. 'The directors pointed out to him that the large outlay of money involved in these purchases would mean that he would need to produce success in the coming season.'

So, given that a few months later it was clear that things had not improved, it was valid to return to the question. Such a review would have been normal practice in any business: a departmental head's performance would be subject to routine scrutiny following a failure to meet targets – and Celtic's target was a trophy every season. But in football, directors cannot get away with taking normal, sensible steps like that. Any whisper of it would have been blown into a crisis (see below!). So, determined to avoid any leak, the Board met secretly at the SFA offices to consider McNeill's position. So tight did we manage to keep this early January meeting, that the Press criticised us for *not* meeting to discuss the crisis!

It was a very sombre Board that convened that evening. Billy's tremendous record as a player and his outstanding success in both his terms as manager weighed heavily. But there was a unanimous feeling that the team simply wasn't going anywhere. Billy had been given a lot of money to spend and it hadn't produced a winning team. The very mention of Martin Hayes led to embarrassment. Hayes had been signed from Arsenal in the summer of 1990 for £650,000. He had appeared only seven times in the first team by the end of January 1991. The only thing that those few appearances did for him was to prove that he wasn't up to the job. In the vernacular, he was a dead loss. If any one factor could be said to have sealed McNeill's fate, it was the signing of Martin Hayes.

The assessment obviously ranged over broader matters. No minutes were taken of the meeting but from notes the clearcut conclusion was that the manager must go. Farrell wanted him to go right away, and McGinn thought that Billy deep down had lost it and wanted out. I was not so sure. I asked: 'Can he retrieve the current situation?' I argued that we had to be sure that the person who came in was demonstrably better than he was. I wasn't convinced that there was a natural successor available. We needed the European place, and the Cup was about to start. Were we likely to be in a better position to achieve these targets with or without McNeill? Very often in football change itself brings short-term improvement, and it was felt that dismissing the manager, though shocking to be implemented in mid-season, might just be the catalyst needed to inspire a good Cup run. Our next game was at home to Aberdeen and an unspoken consensus emerged that, if we lost, Billy would be asked to go.

Celtic beat Aberdeen with a last-minute goal from Tommy Coyne.

A week later, we travelled to Forfar and won a difficult Cup-tie two-nothing. We then drew one-each at Fir Park and beat Dundee United one-nothing at home. The tide of crisis receded and the immediate threat to McNeill was removed. Things were further eased by the intervention of the weather which caused the postponement of a couple of games. We were then into March with a double-header against Rangers looming. No one was going to suggest the immediate removal of the manager now. We won both the Cup-tie against Rangers (the St. Patrick's Day Massacre, although the score was only two-nothing) and the League game in the space of seven days. Everyone was elated.

But the respite was merely temporary. Motherwell knocked us out of the Cup after a semi-final replay. Another blank season, although two hard-fought-for points at Perth in the last game of the season combined with defeat for Dundee United to squeeze us into Europe. We beat St. Johnstone three-two with our first League penalty of the 1990s! Who says we don't have the referees in our pocket?

Cassidy had been critical of the whole way we handled the manager issue. Postponing a decision to see the result of a particular game or because a vital match was coming up seemed to him to be merely procrastination. So he prepared an options paper on how a change of manager might or should be dealt with when it came. Such a document is standard strategic practice in big companies. But we had not asked for one. It just appeared on our desks before a routine Board meeting. A copy also clearly landed on someone else's desk, and copies subsequently found their way to Billy McNeill and, most damagingly, to the *Sun*.

The *Sun* rang me at home on the Friday evening at around six to 'check out rumours' of McNeill's impending departure. From what the reporter asked, I had a growing feeling that he had actually seen a copy of the report, but I dead-batted his questions non-committally. Then he asked if it was true that a draft press release had been prepared and I knew he could only have got that from the Cassidy document – it was the final page.

I phoned Cassidy's home immediately and left a message that he was not to speak to the Press without first ringing me. When he called, I told him of my fears and advised him either to confirm the truth or to say nothing at all. But he refused to believe that the *Sun* had actually got a copy of the options paper. So, against my advice, he challenged the *Sun* to print what they claimed to have got. They did, the following Monday, and got two stories out of it for the price of one.

MEMORANDUM
STRICTLY PRIVATE AND CONFIDENTIAL

To: C.D. White
      J.M. Farrell
      J.C. McGinn
      T.J. Grant
      M. Kelly
      K. Kelly

From: T.F. Cassidy
Date: 24 April 1991

Enclosed are drafts for the procedures for handling the future of the Manager of Celtic Football Club and press release.
 Your swift agreement on them would be appreciated.

T.F. CASSIDY
CHIEF EXECUTIVE

DRAFT
MEMORANDUM

To: Board of Directors
From: T.F. Cassidy
Date: 24 April 1994

If there is to be a change of Manager at Celtic Football Club it is most important that it is handled professionally and with the dignity and pride of all parties protected. The timing of such a move is not as important as how it should be done, although I believe that the longer it is left the less appropriate is the timing. Having said that, a series of meetings must take place and all within a very short period of time. These would be aimed at ending with a decision being taken and an agreed press statement released. These meetings should be as follows:

1. A meeting between the Chief Executive and the Manager to talk about the various options open to the Board in regard to the Manager's future. Most importantly to get the Manager's reaction to the possibility of his leaving the Club and what he would be looking for in the way of compensation.

2. A meeting between the Chief Executive and the Board to enable the Chief Executive to report to the Board on his meeting with the Manager. At this meeting it would also be decided on whether the Manager was going or not and if he was going when and who would be his replacement, temporary or otherwise.

3. A meeting between the Board, the Chief Executive and the Manager. At this meeting, on the assumption the Manager is

leaving then compensation, mutually agreed press statements and scheduling of the release of the information would be agreed. In the event of the decision being that the Manager was to retain his job again agreement should be reached on terms and conditions of a contract and again press releases would have to be agreed and communicated.

4. If the Board decided not to disclose the decision to the Manager at the meeting in (3) then that decision would be communicated to the Manager in another meeting between the Manager and the Chief Executive.

5. The meeting would take place between the Chief Executive and the Assistant Manager to find out whether he would be interested in being a candidate for the Manager's job or not. If he were then terms and conditions would need to be spelt out to him on how that could come about. If he were not it would have to be established whether he would be interested in remaining as a caretaker Manager with a view to returning to the position of an Assistant Manager when a full-time Manager is appointed.

6. Depending upon the outcome of (5) a meeting would take place between the Board, the Chief Executive and the Assistant Manager.

7. Mutually agreed announcements from all parties would be made and any necessary press conferences arranged.

The above, when written on paper, may appear to be lengthy and cumbersome but would all take place within two days and at the very most three days. What is most important, however, is for the Board to decide if they are going to do something and when. For example, if it was agreed that nothing would be done until after the St. Mirren game then all the above could be instituted and completed over a period of 7, 8 and 9 May 1991. Clearly if something were to be done after Mr Bonner's Testimonial then that could be effected on 14, 15 and 16 of May 1991.

T.F. CASSIDY
CHIEF EXECUTIVE

DRAFT PRESS RELEASE

Recently Billy McNeill requested a meeting with the Board of Celtic Football Club to discuss his future as Manager. The Board agreed to his request and a meeting was held on ——. The meeting saw a full and frank exchange of views by everyone concerned and at the end it was decided by mutual agreement that Billy McNeill should leave Celtic Football Club. The agreed severance terms are acceptable to him and indeed he considers them to be extremely fair and generous.

Tommy Craig, the Assistant Manager of Celtic Football Club, has been offered and accepted the position as Caretaker Manager. He has expressed a strong desire to be appointed as the Manager of Celtic Football Club but understands that the position is open for any other candidates who may consider themselves suitable to apply. Clearly Tommy Craig has an opportunity to prove himself as the successor to Billy McNeill because he is already at the Club and working with the players and this should give him slight advantage on any other applicants for the job. He has said that he welcomes the opportunity and would dearly love to become the Manager of Celtic Football Club.

It is in the interests of everyone at the Club, players, supporters that the vacancy is filled on a permanent basis as quickly as possible but the Club also feels that whilst there is a great sense of urgency, a hasty decision will not be taken as it is felt that it is better to take the right decision even if that does take a little while to arrive at.

T.F. CASSIDY
CHIEF EXECUTVE

APPENDUM TO MEMORANDUM (24.4.91)

To: Board of Directors
From: T.F. Cassidy
Date: 24 April 1991

When I sent out my proposals for handling the position of Manager of Celtic Football Club I omitted one point. Would you please add "all the staff of Celtic Football Club including the players should be told about any changes before they read about them, hear of them or see them on television".

T.F. CASSIDY
CHIEF EXECUTIVE

The publication of these documents by the *Sun* was another disastrous indication that Cassidy had yet to appreciate the media appetite for Celtic stories and their lack of scruples in obtaining them. There was nothing at all wrong with the idea of spelling out to a Board that he considered was dithering over the issue exactly what he thought the procedure should be. He was trying to lead the Board through it by the hand. But, given the enemies that he already had and the intense Press interest in the manager's position, there was little chance that the memo would be kept confidential. Cassidy was to discover that Celtic was full of leaks of facts and fiction – but the extent of the treachery astonished him at this moment.

In the event, McNeill's dismissal did not take place until 22 May 1991, but the leak had made it even more of an inevitable decision. The hold-up was temporary, to give McNeill more than a last chance, just because he was Billy McNeill. The Press made a meal of 'the Board's disgraceful treatment of one of Celtic's greatest sons'. But it was the Press leak which created the bad treatment, not the drawing up of an options paper. Newspaper hypocrisy at its worst, as Cassidy kept reiterating.

Cassidy was convinced that the information had been leaked directly from the Board and instituted the usual futile search to find evidence of the culprit. There even emerged the ludicrous suggestion that the directors be required to take lie detector tests, arranged through Glasgow University! Instead, every director had to appear before Chris White and aver that he was not the mole. I don't know who Chris had to swear before. But I had gone into my office to look for my copy of the options paper and couldn't find it. In a state of anxious paranoia (standard kit, remember, for a Celtic director), my gut instinct immediately after I had spoken to the *Sun* was that the leak might have come from my office. Either our cleaner, Mrs Gordon, must have thrown it out with rubbish, where some casual snoop had found it, or it was something more sinister. So I called in security experts to check my systems and effected the changes recommended. Six months later, I found the document in a different file.

Caldwell in his book claims that the document was copied in my office by a member of staff. I don't believe that and, given that I employed thirteen people at the time, it leaves an unfair suspicion over twelve of them. But if it is true, it means that the journalist involved – and possibly the newspaper – handled and published a document which was known to be stolen.

We dismissed McNeill after a Board meeting in May 1991. It was a meeting well-trailed in the Press. The whole Board was present to tell him. We had all agreed we should do this face to face. We had discussed the matter many times, but before McNeill came in we discussed it again – a final *final* review. Then, unbelievably, Farrell changed his mind. 'I think he should be given another year,' he said suddenly. Everybody else was astonished, but everybody else stuck to the plan. We had made it clear to him at the beginning of the season that the money that we had made available just had to produce results. Instead, he had made bad buys. There was no willingness to give him yet more money to waste. Despite pleas to Farrell to make the decision unanimous for the sake of unity, he refused to budge.

After the decision had been taken, I proposed that Billy be given another position within the Club, not a full-time job but one of a consultancy nature. I just could not forget the innumerable, memorable moments this man had given me. He had to be sacked, that was the correct decision – but as the greatest Celt after Jock Stein, he was someone with whom the Club had to maintain a link. The others unanimously rejected the proposal as impractical and it was thrown out.

McNeill strode stiffly into the Boardroom, lacking his usual air of camaraderie. He knew what was coming. Under strain, he had difficulty saying anything. He asked to discuss the terms of his leaving. We all felt terrible. We thanked him for his service to the Club. Then he went to Cassidy to agree a settlement. It was a very satisfactory deal, witnessed by the lack of complaint from McNeill ever since, despite what must have been a sore temptation to speak out during the following painful and controversial years.

Cassidy's infamous options paper had suggested advertising the manager's position to attract candidates. So we did. Tommy Craig was asked to take control in the interim.

From the list of applicants, four were selected for interview: Liam Brady, Frank Stapleton, Ivan Golac and Tommy Craig. The Press, amazingly, did not know of the first three. They were backing Craig. I had a phone call from Wallace Mercer to ask if we were thinking of Joe Jordan! He obviously hadn't got over the stage of being worried by Press rumours. I gladly told him that he could relax. In fact, in the Board's early informal discussions Jordan had been considered and passed over fairly quickly – because of the negative and boring way in which Hearts were playing!

After the interviews, Cassidy advised the Board to think about their choice before finalising an appointment. It was a strong short-leet. Craig was ruled out because he was part of the failed McNeill regime. Golac was very impressive – cool, charming, with tremendous depth of knowledge and experience, but too much of a risk for Celtic at this time, we thought. I liked him and I'm delighted how successful he's become with Dundee United. But I still think that it would have been too big a gamble for us to take in the circumstances. Frank Stapleton, then still a player with Blackburn Rovers, came across as a pleasant, likeable and honest fellow with a superb personality, but too inexperienced. It seemed too early for him to take on such a job – and, indeed, his failure at Bradford confirmed our decision.

Liam Brady was the big name, with glamorous Italian experience, a player who had won trophies in England and the Continent. He was obviously very knowledgeable. A bit introspective for my liking, but he had considerable charm.

Opinion amongst the Board members was evenly divided: McGinn, Chris and I backed Brady, while Grant, Farrell and Kevin preferred Stapleton. Kevin changed his mind to make it Brady. I was pleased. We had made an imaginative and strong appointment, following the arrival of a bold new chief executive. I was immensely optimistic that the Club could now go forward into a new era, despite the lack of unanimity among the directors. All we needed now was a change of luck on the field, and the fans would rally around us.

Liam was told that the aim was to win a trophy next season. He accepted this and he appeared to know exactly what was expected of him. But I now wonder whether he did or not. With hindsight, I think he was shocked at the intensity of feeling in Scotland and of the saturation coverage that Celtic affairs received. It is difficult to believe that the pressure was not as great in Italy; but he was a player there, and a foreigner, which must have helped isolate him just that little bit. I think that he was making his comparisons with England. And I don't think he could believe how seriously and pervasively football was scrutinised up here.

We also talked at the interview about the training of players. I really couldn't believe the few hours that professional footballers in Scotland put in compared with, say, athletes, who train for many more hours every day, or golfers, who come straight from five-hour competitive rounds on to the practice ground. Liam agreed and promised to improve the training schedules and to concentrate on improving ball skills. One successful tactic Liam introduced early on was mounting a counter-attack from opponents' corners kicks. I raised this at one Board meeting, complimenting Liam on its success. Then I asked what our plans were if an opposing team decided to use our tactic against us. It hadn't even been envisaged. One particular question I asked him concerned Paul McStay. As every Celtic supporter knows, Paul McStay's shooting is somewhat erratic. I asked Liam if he could work on that to develop the potential of a talented player and he promised he would. Either he didn't or it didn't work, because McStay still can't shoot for toffee.

It was a few days before we could parade Brady in front of the Press. It was one of the biggest media circuses seen at Celtic Park, and he was well received. I was, for the first time since I'd joined the Board just a year earlier, content enough. It was, after all, another new start.

Liam Brady was given a £2 million budget to spend on players immediately. Tony Cascarino and Gary Gillespie were his choices. Cascarino was a failure, but at least Liam managed to swap him for Tommy Boyd who, while not a total disaster, was certainly not worth the £1 million Liam spent on Cascarino. And we wanted a forward, not a back. Gillespie, as every Scotland supporter knew, was injury-prone. They were bad buys, an opinion which everyone shared with me even before we had seen them perform. Some have asked me why the Board sanctioned them, if it was that obvious. But a football club director is pretty powerless in such matters – at least in formal Board meetings. If you blocked the purchases, the manager would rightly point to your action in any subsequent lack of success. Managers are paid handsomely. They have to survive on their own hunches. If they fail, they go. It's as simple as that. Just weeks into a new managership, failure was not yet on the agenda.

But there was still the underlying external hostility. Looking back, it is easy to imagine a carefully thought-out plan. The reality, I suspect, was that the opposition opportunistically took advantage out of every adverse situation – usually one produced, directly or indirectly, by a bad result on the field. Throughout the season there were rumblings from box-holders and sponsors. In June 1991, the existence of an alleged Weisfeld/McCann bid was discovered; and as the Press continued to snipe at Celtic, so Cassidy continued to snipe at the Press, culminating in a three-page attack in the *Celtic View* in June, just before Liam Brady was appointed.

While leaks and stories of the discontent of various groups with the Board continued, Dempsey ostensibly kept aloof. He did address the inaugural meeting of 'Save Our Celts' in June, where he 'made it very clear that he was not in favour of boycotts'. On a fans' phone-in, he said: 'I do not wish to further destabilise Celtic in any way whatsoever. My message to Celtic fans is "Keep supporting the team".'

Cassidy's strategy appeared to be to take all the heat off the individual directors, and to stand in the kitchen alone. It was, in essence, a negative strategy – perhaps valuable in the short term, given the lack of unanimity among the directors, but ultimately doomed to make matters worse.

After investigation of the options, Cassidy confirmed Michael Kelly Associates as Celtic's PR consultants at a basic fee of £250 per week plus 'overtime', later to be capped by David at £375 per week including expenses, but I never charged my own hours. On 14 March 1991, on our recommendation, Cassidy agreed to try a new, more user-friendly approach to the media. From 5 April 1991 we were asked to arrange weekly Press briefing meetings for him. These were widely welcomed by astonished hacks, but they didn't last more than four weeks. Cassidy had decided that confrontation with the Press was the best approach to see them off. His outspoken comments always attracted unwanted headlines. Off the record remarks seemed guaranteed to raise further controversies.

Towards the end of April, Cassidy announced the results of a market research survey into the views and desires of Celtic fans. They were broadly ignored by the media which were more interested in the dispute between the Club and Paul Elliott over the matter of his housing. Elliott was one of two Celtic players (the other was Charlie Nicholas) who got into a fankle as a result of involvement with a complex tax-avoiding, profit-making, house purchase scheme produced for them by Brian Dempsey before he was a director. Cassidy took a tough public stance over Elliott's claims. Predictably, the media made an anti-Celtic meal of it, and Cassidy blew his top.

Players are always looking for ways to squeeze the last penny out of their contracts. In particular, they have an even greater resentment than the rest of us to paying tax. Chris refused adamantly to get involved in any dodgy tricks. Dempsey, advising McGinn at the time, came up with a plan. As part of a player contract, he would build and sell a house to the player. The player would then sell the house at the end of his three-year contract making a tax-free gain. Fine, if prices kept rising; and if they didn't, the first agreement that was concluded (before I came on the Board) provided that the Club would make good the short-fall between the £100,000 profit expected and the actual amount. Paul Elliott moved into his house for eleven days, sold it and asked to see McGinn. He told the chairman that he had only made £7,000 profit and could he have the other £93,000, please. When the agreement was checked, it was discovered that it had omitted to oblige Elliott to hold the house for any particular period. That was what led to the court case and the out-of-court settlement.

Charlie Nicholas's problem was slightly different. He never got round to selecting the plot of land on which the house could be built within the specified period – but he still wanted the profit of £100,000 that he was told that he would have made. He was offered an ex gratia payment of £25,000 at the end of his contract, or when he left if that was earlier. He turned this down, the Press found out and Celtic were still arguing about it when I left.

There are possible tax implications in schemes such as these which the Inland Revenue decided to investigate in 1992. Among many matters currently under the microscope is Paul Elliott's transfer from Pisa. This occurred before I was a director but I understand that Pisa insisted that part of the £675,000 transfer fee be paid in cash. So McGinn went down to the bank with officials from the Italian club, drew out £175,000 in cash and handed it over! However now the Inland Revenue is questioning exactly who were present at the bank that day in July 1989.

The other transfer which I now know is being questioned is the even earlier one of Andy Walker from Motherwell in 1987. Celtic increased the transfer fee by £25,000 which Motherwell then paid to the player. Celtic indemnified Motherwell from any future liability to pay tax on the money.

When the Inland Revenue investigation was revealed to the Board, the directors who had been on the Board at the relevant time insisted that everything had been conducted properly and that there would be no liability falling on the Club. If the circumstances were as described by them then there was no reason to make a provision earlier, nor was one made in the 1993 accounts.

On 13 May 1991 Mike Stanger wrote the following letter to Cassidy, without my knowledge:

Dear Terry,
I enclose further transcripts from Saturday's programmes on radio, which make rather depressing reading.

In the case of any other client, I would be recommending an executive media training course, but it has been difficult for me to assess to what extent the high-profile of the past few months has been part of your 'grand plan' for transforming the fortunes of Celtic F.C., or how much of this has taken you as well as me by surprise!

Should the latter be the case, and should you be interested in a media training course (cost: around £700), I would be happy to arrange it.

As a former BBC producer, I am well aware myself of the unpredictable nature of journalists. Nevertheless, I remain, as ever, available to advise you whenever needed, and if possible in advance!

Yours sincerely,

(Mike Stanger)
Senior Consultant

There is no reply in the file.

The bad PR continued into the start of the next season, with the disclosure of a petty row between Cassidy and Brady. Not the start we wanted.

We didn't get the start we wanted on the field, either. Airdrie put us out of the Skol Cup on penalties in September 1991. Liam's reaction was the first sign that he didn't really understand the demands made on Celtic by our fans.

I was lunching in the Cheese Cake Factory in Rodeo Drive, Beverly Hills, just as the team bus was pulling out of Broomfield. I phoned home for the result and spoiled my meal. In fact, the news spoiled the next few days of my holiday.

I was speechless when I came home to review the papers and to find that Liam had exonerated his players. This showed how out of touch he was then. In England, big teams do lose Cup matches, and this apparently is acceptable. But in Scotland Celtic simply cannot be beaten in Cup competition by minnows. His reaction seriously affected his credibility with the fans and with me. Well after the result I told him how I felt, and I think to a certain extent he got the message. But I don't know that he was ever entirely convinced about how seriously he had to take it.

He was taught another lesson in Switzerland. We had drawn Xamax Neuchatel in the UEFA Cup, a team we should have beaten easily. Liam must have thought so as well, because he committed the team to a policy of attack, which was tantamount to committing suicide. They won five-one, our worst European defeat. Despite that, if Nicholas had scored with an early penalty in the second leg, we still might have got through, so bad were they. But he missed. The Boardroom problems were clearly worrying him even then.

Off the field, the most important task to be tackled by Cassidy was the stadium question and, in my view, Cassidy did exactly the right thing. He called in external experts to present options. There were any number of varieties of proposals for the re-development of Celtic Park. None of them, though, attacked the fundamental problem of the location, in the middle of a run-down part of Glasgow with practically no modern transport or other infra-structure available. Bits of undeveloped land in surrounding areas were in so many different hands it would have taken years to assemble enough for a decent-sized car park, let alone a new stadium complex – and how would it all be paid for? Dempsey had proposed a bold scheme for a greenfield development with associated commercial ventures at Robroyston, but it was never clear how it would have been paid for. And without a financial plan any proposal was ill-advised.

In due course a way forward emerged. Cassidy was impressed by the forward-thinking and imaginative ideas of two groups (Superstadia and York Trust) who approached the Club. One was basically suggesting a property-development route like Dempsey's, the other was arriving at the same conclusions from a financial starting point. With Cassidy's encouragement, the two groups came together, and in May 1991 the Club appointed them to investigate stadium feasibility options.

The joint group's first task was to conduct what nobody had ever undertaken for Celtic, despite a decade or more of clear need – a proper, level-headed, independent, detailed and costed investigation of potential sites for a new stadium complex in the Glasgow area. The sites to be investigated were to include Celtic Park itself and Robroyston, to ensure that we were not biasing ourselves against the obvious. Superstadia appointed Professor Gwyn Kennedy, a prominent and respected Renfrew-based town planner, to do the investigation work. A sensible, approachable man, he had been associated with a proposal for a football stadium at Linwood, so had a clear grasp of the issues. He listed fifteen potential sites around the city, and said it would take six months to come up with the conclusions of his work.

The group reported back in September 1991 with a short-leet of five sites. Cassidy let it be known that a final decision would be made in the spring – a needless hostage to fortune.

Nevertheless, things were at last beginning to move in the right direction. But Chris and I still needed to consolidate our voting strength. Chris had the share-power, but important decisions could still be scuppered by whimsical foolishness in the Boardroom. We needed to change the balance on the Board in our favour. One way to do this was to introduce a new face.

Various businessmen were discussed, Gerald Weisfeld being one. Gerard Eadie of C R Smith was out of the question, following an inept row with Cassidy. Brian Gilda of the Peoples Ford dealerships was definitely interested, but the Board weren't convinced. The matter dragged on through the autumn into the new year. And all the time, it became more and more obvious that whatever was discussed in the Boardroom was being relayed to people outside.

Now it seemed clear that we needed alliances within the Board to safeguard the voting power. Chris still felt the disloyalty that McGinn had exhibited in his support of Dempsey and was no longer willing to rely on him. So we decided that Kevin should become chairman in McGinn's place. Kevin's appointment was part of the necessary bridge-building with him and Grant. Most of them may have thought I would move to become chairman, a thought no doubt planted in their minds by the rebels, as they were now indelibly tagged by the Press. (That label was almost the only positive PR achievement of our defence campaign, given that they themselves preferred the title, 'concerned shareholders'.) I suppose there was a remote possibility that I might have become chairman, but I didn't really consider the option. Kevin's appointment was an effective way to remove any doubts about my ambitions. And I had no intention of upstaging Kevin. He was my cousin.

Chris simply told McGinn he was to go. McGinn asked if a deal could be arranged because, incredibly, he didn't have a pension. Eventually, it was agreed that his £40,000 salary could be reduced to just £25,000 instead of the non-executive directors' normal level of £2,500. In October 1991, Kevin was duly installed. There was a detectable relaxation within the Board, and relief that it was not me!

Having made our position more secure in the Boardroom, there remained the struggle to ensure that we did not lose control of our shareholding majority. With Chris's very powerful holding, we did not need many other supporters beyond our immediate families. But it was clear to me that shares would begin to change hands, and I thought that we should be the first into the market. Celtic shares had never been traded before, simply because the holders regarded them as beyond value. They were family heirlooms, to be held in trust and handed down. But with this tradition now three and four generations old, with the holdings being split up between more and more people, and with many shareholders losing contact with the Club, the bonds were becoming weaker.

I knew that Dempsey had been courting shareholders and I knew that Chris and I had to move fast. By chance, one Irish shareholder had written to me as early as 1990 and when I had followed it up I found that she was quite willing to sell. Knowing the commotion that it would cause, I had not taken the matter any further. Now I put it to Chris that we should, between us, buy enough shares to ensure our independence from everyone. He would not countenance such an idea which he felt strongly was against the Celtic way.

I could not move him on this, even when another major shareholder, Maureen Blackburn, approached me. Her story was one which must have reflected that of many. She saw the power struggle building up and was aware that approaches were being made to buy shares. She was not rich and had always set her heart on buying a holiday home in Italy. She wanted enough money from her shares to allow her to do this. As there were 800 shares involved, I urged Chris to let me buy them. He refused: 'We are not going to start that. Let them, if they want.'

They had already begun.

Chapter Seven

To do ought good never will be our task,
But ever to do ill our sole delight . . .

Paradise Lost, 1.157

The role of the media in the struggle for Celtic's soul is one that deserves a treatise of its own. Since Watergate, journalists have been increasingly aware of their power to alter others' destinies. Many of them go to great lengths to emulate Woodward and Bernstein, in the political field principally, but increasingly so in all areas of modern life, from monarchy to business, from sport to personal scandal. Unfortunately most of them ignore the painstaking methods of the mainstream American Press and their obsession with checking allegations with at least two sources before publication. Little wonder that Howard Kurtz, the media correspondent of the *Washington Post*, was moved recently to deplore the poor reporting standards in Britain.

The Scottish sporting Press showed few inhibitions in publishing rumours, half-truths and distortions about Celtic. Indeed, that is what most of the coverage consisted of. It is fascinating to see McCann, who was swept to power with hysterical media rejoicing, complaining, only two months into the job, about 'guesswork and speculation'. 'We can only deal in hard news,' was his naïve plea. He will find no such wimpish restriction on Press freedom here. Freedom here means freedom to publish what you like, true or not, checked or unchecked, with no right of reply offered to the target.

Like anyone happy to be living in a Western democracy, I am totally committed to the concept of a free Press. But in the UK that is something we do not have. To me, a free Press reports consistently and objectively, covering fairly the different aspects of a story. Editorialising is clearly identified as such and separated from the factual elements of the story. Pretty basic stuff.

Here the Press follow lines dictated by proprietors, which is why its political coverage is so distorted. And the driving force of newspapers and of commercial television and radio is profits, not truth. No wonder they react with savagery to any criticism.

The Celtic story is so trivial in UK media terms that its coverage is certain to have made little impact in London; however, those considering sensible limitations to the damage our unfettered Press currently does, could do worse than to use it as a case study of worst practice.

In the case of Celtic, I am not suggesting there was a proprietor or editor dictating an anti-Board line as a point of principle. Of course, there wasn't. But Celtic was seen as a good story, that is, one that sold papers. So any trivia which filled space was included, accurate or not. Indeed, the more sensational it was the better. The Celtic team was not producing results on the field, the fans were disillusioned and they wanted to read criticism of the Board. That is what the Press gave them, fair or not, whether it was based on fact or fiction.

In addition, certain journalists chose very early on to side with the rebels. In many cases, those journalists are now described by their colleagues as 'Celtic supporters'. Fed up with Celtic living in the shadow of Rangers, on and off the field, these fans with word processors were prepared to support anyone who promised change. This led them into claims on the ludicrous side of hyperbole. Like dubbing every potential takeover-bidder a millionaire: people like Jim Doherty, who honestly plies his trade as a second-hand yacht salesman in Toronto. Even to the quality press he was a 'millionaire', a 'tycoon'. To the tabloids he was 'mega-bucks Doherty'.

Journalists were assiduously and shamelessly courted in a way which they would condemn as indecent behaviour from any self-respecting public relations company. Journalists would have themselves described what went on as 'secret meetings' and 'smear plots'.

Two of the Board's most severe critics, Kevin McCarra and Gerry McNee, are thanked in Low's book; and Dempsey wrote the foreword to Caldwell's book. Surely this must give their editors cause for some second thoughts about balance and objectivity? Because what I am criticising is the lack of editorial control that was exercised in the Celtic story.

Every person who deals with the media has his or her own

favourite journalist, whom they trust and to whom they divulge information both on and off the record. Any good journalist would have been delighted to have, and would rightly have nurtured, a source in the rebel camp and would have written up the stories thus obtained. They might even justifiably be driven to comment. But that comment should clearly have been labelled as such and the other point of view given equal space or opportunity. That did not happen. Inaccurate reports were published without being checked with Celtic – and when we followed their publication with rebuttals and retractions, they rarely appeared.

Gerry McNee, who long before 1990 had put on record his low esteem for the Celtic Board, clearly made up his mind that Dempsey was the only person in the universe who could pull the Club through the mess into which it had got itself. No doubt suitably encouraged and with a regular flow of leaked information being fed direct to his doorstep, he continued his quite deliberate campaign of denigration of the Celtic Board, later of Cassidy and, after the Board changes had been effected, he turned his attentions to Lou Macari.

McNee not only admits campaigning against the Celtic Board, but is proud of it. There must, of course, be room for principled campaigning journalism and for journalists who adopt an exclusive point of view. Certainly, it must be difficult for a journalist to resist building up his name and career on the back of a hot story. The astonishing thing about McNee's campaign, however, was that none of the media for which he worked felt it necessary to strike any balance. Given the recent track record of newspapers over a whole series of topics, this might be all that one could expect from them, though this should be no excuse. But it is a sinister development that Scottish Television allowed itself to be used as a platform to promote only one side of the story. It is still amazing to me that Scottish Television, charged as it is by Act of Parliament to be impartial and fair and hedged about with regulations to that effect, consistently refused my requests for balance.

As a specific example of the treatment we got, Cassidy complained to Scottish Television about McNee's treatment of the Celtic deal with its kit suppliers. There were three competing companies, and McNee had chosen to back the wrong one. On his Friday night spot, he told the nation how

Above left: James Kelly, the author's grandfather and Celtic's first signing. He later became chairman until his death in 1931.

Above right: Sir Robert Kelly, the author's uncle and Celtic chairman from 1947 to 1971, pictured with Jock Stein and Billy McNeill.
(Herald Picture Library)

Kevin Kelly, pictured in April 1992 with plans for the new stadium at the Cambuslang site.
(Herald Picture Library)

Brian Dempsey and Fergus McCann briefing the Press.
(Herald Picture Library)

David Low and Fergus McCann leaving the bank, 4 March 1994.
(Herald Picture Library)

A Celtic line-up away from home. *front row*: Farrell, McGinn, Smith and Kevin Kelly *middle row*: Cassidy, Grant, the author and Chris White *back row*: Jack Mulhearon, George Douglas, Maureen Kelly, Zita Kelly and Francis McCrossin.
(Herald Picture Library)

Donald Smith outlines plans to the press and media for the proposed Cambuslang Stadium as Kevin Kelly looks on, February 1994.
(Herald Picture Library)

Ariel view of intended development at Cambuslang, as
submitted for planning permission in 1992.
(Herald Picture Library)

Artist's impression of the stadium interior.
(Herald Picture Library)

Leaving McDiarmid Park
following Celtic's defeat
by St Johnstone in October
1993. An eventful occasion,
it was also Liam Brady's last
match as Celtic manager.
(Herald Picture Library)

The author delivers a Press statement announcing
Lou Macari's appointment as Celtic manager.
(Herald Picture Library)

Farewell to the Jungle.

Vincent the Parrot had his wings clipped whilst trying to visit Paul McStay at the Bon Secours clinic. *(Studio Cee)*

The author with Chris White at Firhill.
(Herald Picture Library)

the deal with this company had fallen through and what the terrible consequences would be for the Club. On the following Tuesday, we announced the deal with Umbro which Cassidy had put together. It was the biggest ever kit deal in British football history, worth (conservatively) £11 million to the Club over eight years. The following Friday, McNee rubbished the deal and said it had been hurriedly put together in the wake of the collapse of negotiations with the other company. The truth was that the Umbro deal had been signed the previous Friday morning. Naturally, McNee had made no contact with us to check the facts. But he had contacted Umbro, and asked them a series of leading – or rather misleading – questions, designed to shore up his gaffe. This was the standard of coverage of Celtic affairs which journalists, too, were to inflict on the whole Celtic saga. Throughout it all, Scottish Television's management acted the innocent bystanders.

Protests to Gus McDonald, managing director of Scottish Television, were always dealt with by line managers anxious to impress their boss by defending the company's integrity. The whole truth about Celtic and fairness in reporting were definitely casualties in this matter at Scottish Television.

Once, however, an alternative Celtic view did get airtime – in the famous edition of *Sport in Question* in which McNee for the first time appeared flustered as fans questioned his motives. He said: 'I am on record a number of times since Brian Dempsey left the Board as saying it was a major mistake by Celtic. I think you will find a lot of people in the media would like to see him there because they feel he has the quality . . . I try to do my job as passionately as I can because I believe it is important . . .' Then he launched into a tirade in which he claimed 'a major person associated with Celtic has made a quite blatant attempt to have a go at my professional abilities . . . . my right to earn a living. My lawyer is looking at this seriously at the moment. A file is being prepared.'

Liam Brady was on the show too, and he challenged McNee about another factually incorrect and unchecked story he'd put out the previous Friday, about an injury to Tony Mowbray. McNee was backed into a corner, and the following Friday the allegation was withdrawn. On *Sport in Question* there was the ludicrous incident when he hauled a persistently critical questioner out of the audience to the platform, flourished the

1935/36 Cup Final medal which had been won by Jimmy McGrory, and told the unfortunate witness: 'You are a very privileged man.'

The 'quality' Press was no better; the *Scotsman* carried as many factual inaccuracies as any other paper. Hugh Keevins interrupted a match report to tell us that the bank were now demanding monthly reports. 'Not so,' I told him. 'A shareholder told me,' he said. 'Why didn't you check it with me?' I asked. Silence. And no correction. In another article, he claimed that David Smith had been the only director to pay for his shares and therefore the only one who deserved compensation, when it had been a matter of controversy that I had bought shares (£40,000 worth) at the time of the EGM in March 1992.

There were many other specific examples of factual inaccuracies that could easily have been checked. More than once, I brought them to the attention of Magnus Linklater, former editor of the *Scotsman*. He wasn't interested. His view was that sports reporters, in particular, needed stories. He said that 'Keevins is getting plenty from the other side. If you don't give him something, he'll just use their stuff. Give him stories and he'll be quite happy to use them.' It didn't seem to matter if they were true or not. Would Linklater have reacted in the same way about his business page journalists? And, of course, Keevins still never checked anything with me. In contrast to the *Scotsman*, Radio Clyde made Keevins correct his mistakes – sometimes, anyway.

So here we had two of the most powerful figures in journalism in Scotland refusing to allow the Celtic Board the protection of balance, objectivity and the whole truth.

Meanwhile, Cassidy was starting to rage around the Celtic china shop, taking on all-comers like a prize fighter. He incensed the Rangers hierarchy when he allowed himself to respond deprecatingly to media questioning about their shining newly re-developed stadium. A gift-wrapped sensation for newspapers, although what he actually said was no more than the truth, namely that Ibrox had gone about as far as it could go in terms of the exploitation of its site.

Cassidy also got embroiled in an argument over the renewal of Paul McStay's contract – a small example of how Cassidy's attempts to introduce some rationality into the system were thwarted. The player's contract was up in the summer of

1992. In January, Cassidy told Brady that he would like an early indication from the player as to what his intentions were. Sensible management to allow forward planning, you would think. But this is football, and business cannot be allowed to interfere. Liam didn't like this approach and resisted it. McStay was naturally unhappy, as it called for him to make a decision. The Press got the story and they certainly were not going to let Cassidy win, even though one of their campaign themes was for a more business-like approach at Celtic Park.

In my mind, there is no doubt that we could have negotiated a much better contract with McStay. Everyone wanted to keep him, not so much because we thought he was worth the money but because of the public impact of his departing. So towards the end of the season we made him an extremely generous offer, then, after we had given him a reasonable time to consider it, Liam was asked to establish whether or not he intended to re-sign. At the next Board meeting, Brady reported on his talk with McStay and told us that he had arranged to hear his answer that very morning.

Liam left the meeting to speak to the player. He came back and told us that McStay had decided not to re-sign. Rather, he wanted to consider his options. McStay also asked that this should not be publicised, whereas we wanted to announce the factual position – that he had turned down an exceptional offer.

Liam was sent to tell McStay this. He took longer than we expected, so I went to hurry him up. When I got into the manager's room, there was McStay sitting in his training kit, looking downcast. I went to him, told him that I had heard his decision, thanked him for what he had done for us and wished him all the best – a fairly normal repsonse to a long-serving employee who has decided to move on. He wasn't expecting that at all and looked up in horror. It was quite clear from his reaction and demeanour that his heart was not in a move. I went back to the Boardroom and told the other directors that, as far as I was concerned, McStay didn't intend going anywhere. I reiterated this when Liam came back and suggested that he now privately withdraw the offer to the player. Apart from it being crystal clear that McStay had no stomach for a move, it was also obvious that there really wasn't anyone that anxious to buy him. After a few weeks had gone past he would have been much easier to negotiate with. Liam rejected this strategy and left the offer on the table. Indeed, when McStay came back, having run out of options, the offer might even have been improved marginally. No way to run a business or to gain the respect of employees.

It was a similar situation when the John Collins contract came up for renewal. An initial offer was rejected, but again Liam refused to withdraw it and the player was able to keep the Club hanging around while he made sure that there was nothing better elsewhere.

Internal problems such as these were exacerbated by our awareness of the impending coalition of forces opposed to Celtic's ruling dynasties which had been coming together throughout the last months of 1991. The extent of the plot was revealed when David Low, by now a self-styled 'football analyst', proposed a radical financial solution to Celtic's problems. In *Scotland on Sunday*, Frank Shennan, Low's business colleague, and another journalist, Kevin McCarra, a Celtic supporter, exclusively announced that 'a secret bid . . . by a group of businessmen' to 'overhaul' Celtic had been launched. Their thesis was that the Club, compared to other similar-sized businesses, was undercapitalised. A consortium had been formed, we were told, with the support of some of the minority shareholders, to call an EGM and take over the Club. The Club's share-structure had indeed been virtually unchanged since the 1890s – but this wasn't a call for modernity. It was a takeover bid.

Low called for the Club to 'go public' to bring in the additional £16 million of capital they believed a business of Celtic's standing needed for trading in the 1990s. If implemented, of course, this would almost certainly mean the dilution of existing shareholdings, as none of the Board was personally rich enough to buy the additional shares required to preserve their voting power. And once the Club had 'gone public' nothing could stop any rich individual from taking over the Club at any time, able to brush aside a hundred years of tradition at a whim. The experience of football clubs in England, such as Newcastle United or Tottenham Hotspur, did not provide a happy expectation of benefit from the strategy.

Although it was undeniably true that the Club was under-capitalised, those who made the simplistic appeal for shares in a private Celtic company to be made available for anyone, including fans, to purchase, had not thought the question through. It would have been irresponsible to invite fans to make what would have been an emotional investment which lacked marketability. Ask the many Hibs fans who lost money when they bought their Club's shares whether they would recommend such a scheme. Quite simply, with private Celtic shares fans would not have found it easy to realise their investment, for example in an emergency. I went on record at the time as saying that fans should in principle be allowed to buy shares, but I could devise no practical way of achieving this or of preventing the shares from being concentrated in too few hands. The plan which David developed would have overcome these drawbacks by linking the shares to a valuable real asset, namely the new stadium proposed for Cambuslang. The value of Cambuslang was sufficiently large to justify a public company with a wide institutional shareholding and an active daily market in the shares.

Faced with our implacable opposition to his thesis, David Low added to his credentials as a financial and corporate mercenary by embracing the man whom he had publicly denounced in his letter to the *Glasgow Herald* just months earlier. He started to help Dempsey to lobby shareholders in an attempt to build a majority. It was obvious from the arithmetic that to win they needed the support of a number of directors. Farrell, as Dempsey's lawyer, was always likely to be on his side, but he was not enough, having very few shares. They needed Grant or Kevin. McGinn continued to toe the line, as promised, but it could be assumed he would bend with the wind. Our search for the right person to join the Board came to a head just as Dempsey and his crowd were girding their loins to call the EGM in March 1992.

Ever since I had been co-opted to the Board, Chris had been in touch with David Smith. The architect of Europe's biggest-ever takeover deal (of the Gateway Supermarket Group), David brought a breadth and depth to the Board in precisely the area where we had been criticised as weakest – business acumen. He also was and is the complete Celtic supporter, travelling from London once and twice a week for games.

Chris and I had met David in the middle of 1991 in an attempt to persuade him to become a director. I also saw him as someone who could fund the purchase of shares that I saw we had to make. But he was very reluctant to take up either offer. He seemed to feel that, with just over 50% of the shares, we had enough, and that the worst possible position for the rebels was for them to have 49% and lose. To me, that did not leave enough margin for error. It also meant we had to rely on too many people.

David also resisted our appeal to him to join the Board. I never discussed this reluctance with him, but understood that his business colleagues in London were horrified that he should get involved with anything as unproductive and as volatile as a football club.

Amid reports of meetings held over the winter of 1991-92 in North America, Ireland and Scotland, Dempsey admitted in February 1992 he 'had been approached' by Canadian 'yacht broker' Jim Doherty and Low. Not for the first or last time, he feigned a lack of interest to the *Daily Record*. In the *Scotsman* the same day, Tom Grant more or less admitted he knew of the dealings going on behind the scenes. 'I am not saying that I am not involved in this business, and I am not saying that I am.' As ever, Grant had it both ways. Two days later, the *Sun* reported that Dempsey had the support of Grant and Farrell to change the Board.

Doherty and Low met Kevin and demanded representation on the Board. They didn't tell him they were secretly taping the conversation. The campaign leading up to the EGM was now in full swing, with the pedlars of disinformation and baseless speculation in full tow:

14 February – *Scotsport*: Doherty says he wants on the Board and to remove Chris and me. He wants Dempsey back. McNee suggests an EGM could be called if Celtic go out of the Cup.

15 February – *Sun*: 'Mega-bucks' Jim Doherty claims nearly 50% backing. He will remove Michael Kelly and Chris White and bring back Brian Dempsey.

16 February – *Scotland on Sunday*: Doherty close to seat on Celtic Board. Prediction that Low and Doherty will join the Board. Rebels claim 47.5%, including the votes of Grant, Farrell and McGinn.

18 February – *Scottish Daily Express*: McNee's column poses Kevin Kelly as the man who could swing the vote, so treats him

gently: 'Kevin Kelly is a quiet man who has always shunned the limelight and controversy, and now finds himself holding the balance of power. His hour has come. What will he do?'

18 February – *Glasgow Herald*: One rebel says 'there could be blood on the walls'. This enables Dempsey to eschew anything which turns the 'spotlight on personalities rather than issues' in statesmanlike terms.

18 February – *Evening Times*: Dempsey announces planning permission to build 800 houses at Robroyston. 'I have received the planning permission the Celtic Board said I would never get.' I had, of course, reported to the Board in 1990 that planning permission for housing could readily be obtained. It was the other developments which would have been problematic.

19 February – *Scotsman*: An EGM will now be called to challenge the right of the existing Board to continue guiding the Club. Rebels will guarantee £15 million and raise £5 million from fans. Michael McDonald will put up £1 million.

19 February – BBC Radio Scotland: Jim Craig comments on the possible takeover and the EGM.

21 February – *Daily Record*: Jim Craig revealed as the rebels' Mr Fixit who has been secretly contacting Celtic shareholders to buy their shares or proxies.

The BBC, to their credit, took just twenty-four hours to decide to dispense with Craig's services, an action Celtic never sought despite accusations to the contrary.

On the day the unfortunate Mr Fixit was unmasked, we announced the appointment of a new Board member. David Smith had at last decided to marry his attachment with his business judgement – even though there was going to be nothing in this for him.

We took the Board totally by surprise with our nomination of David. With Kevin's support, Chris and I simply forced it through. This prompted Grant to tell BBC Television that a proposal for the co-option of Doherty and Low to the Celtic Board had been lost on a casting vote, and that he had proposed the return of Dempsey to the Board, supported by Farrell. He claimed not to know anything about Smith, but later had to admit that the Board had interviewed him a year earlier. During the Board meeting, McGinn confirmed that he had met David a number of years previously and that he had shown detailed knowledge of Celtic's history. But McGinn wondered if he had mugged it up for that meeting!

The following day, the aspect of David Smith which excited more comment than anything else was that he was a Protestant – so much for serious and opinion-forming journalism in the West of Scotland! Even Alf Young in the *Herald* mentioned it, and on the front page too. Despite the intense hostility Grant felt towards David, this was never a factor for him.

The following day, when the rebels threatened a Court of Session move to block David's appointment (a move which never came), Dempsey also confirmed he had spent £250,000 on buying shares and proxies. The buying price of what had been £2 shares was now said to be £165. In any other business, this would have been signalled the true worth of the assets. In the case of Celtic, it was a value that was ignored when takeovers were proposed.

David stepped into this cauldron of whipped-up media hysteria with astonishing *sangfroid*. Here was one of the most spectacularly successful Scottish businessmen of his era being treated as if he was a nobody, while those who misleadingly exuded the aura of success were being treated like gods and saviours.

After his initial hesitation, David entered into his duties at Celtic Park with great enthusiasm. The evening before his appointment, I had introduced Cassidy to him. Cassidy was very suspicious, and afterwards told me that he knew then that David's appointment meant the end for him. That night, he asked to be made a director. I agreed that the logic of business organisation dictated that, as chief executive, he should be. But Chris vehemently opposed the idea, telling Cassidy that he must prove himself first.

David's appointment was a major step in the right direction, but still more had to be done about the appalling situation at Board level. Nothing meaningful could be discussed in that forum. It might as well have been broadcast. There was no trust on which to base progress out of the mess. We had to act decisively so we called the EGM ourselves to remove Grant and Farrell, thereby wrong-footing the rebels. But we did not know the extent of Grant's duplcity, for it has now been revealed that as early as November 1991 he was on the rebels' side and by February 1992 was working as part of the rebel team.

Kevin Kelly wrote in sad terms to the shareholders:

All of us can be in no doubt that, at this time, Celtic faces critical decisions that will determine the future direction of the Club, and the success of the team for the foreseeable future. In such circumstances, it is essential that your Board of Directors is agreed and united on the policies and strategy that must be pursued.

'Sadly, this is not the case. The events of the past few weeks demonstrate that there is a body of opinion that seeks to alter the structure and composition of the Board.

'In an attempt to bridge the gap, I proposed the co-option of David Smith. David, a Scot and a Celtic supporter, is a chartered accountant with a sound financial track record. He masterminded, in 1989, the £2.5 billion acquisition of the Gateway supermarket group – the biggest merger in Europe of the 1980s. He is exactly the calibre of person that shareholders, fans and commentators have been seeking to strengthen the Board.

'My proposal, though eventually carried on my casting vote, was resisted by some directors. Further, despite my pleas, two insisted on making their dissent public in such manner as to destroy any working relationship that might have existed on the Board.

'There is now continuing talk of further proposals for change. The atmosphere of uncertainty that this has created is clearly interfering with the proper running of your Company.

'These conflicts at Board level must be resolved at the earliest possible time; in order to allow a coherent and agreed strategy to emerge.

'Therefore an Extraordinary General Meeting of the Company is being called, to confirm and approve the appointment of David Smith as a director, and to remove from the Board James T Farrell and Thomas J Grant.

'I enthusiastically recommend the endorsement of David Smith to you. I also trust that I will have your support for the further changes proposed above. These are essential because your Board must have a clear and united vision of the future.

'Chris White, Michael Kelly and I have had specific ideas on the strategy which must be followed and the fundamental changes that must be made in the running of the Club if Celtic is to respond effectively to the challenges that we face. The pressure that we have felt, to attempt to maintain unity on the Board and to avoid public wrangling, has meant that, up until now, we have not been able to bring these plans forward.

'But, now that other directors have made public their opposition to us and to the way we want to work, we have the opportunity of placing the resolution of the matter before shareholders.

The following day Grant told Radio Clyde, morosely, that he was seeking a solution to avoid the EGM. Archie McPherson's comment was: 'That sounds like a man who has backed a loser and wants off the hook.'

McNee called Grant 'spineless' and said, if the axe fell on his head, Kelly and White would be doing Celtic a big favour. Farrell, he said, should resign. After the EGM, with Grant seen as the key to toppling Chris and me, McNee said: 'No one can doubt Grant's genuine love of Celtic and his commitment to the Club, which has sometimes been misdirected and even a little misguided . . . now that the EGM is over, he must harness his energies in the right direction. If things go wrong, he must come out all guns blazing and tell the fans and the media exactly what is going on.'

In fact, I do not think that Grant fully appreciated the dangers that faced him in courting the rebels. He always persisted in the naïve view that we should all be working together 'for the good of Celtic', ignoring the fact that the rebels wanted us out and that Dempsey was involved in a crusade of revenge. There were two sides and he tried to stay on both. By and large, he succeeded.

He would certainly do anything to avoid losing his seat. The week before the EGM, Brian Gilda of Peoples asked me if I'd meet him and Grant. When they came into my office I told him that if he had not sought the meeting I would have sought him out, as I too thought that there must be a better solution. I was glad to see Grant because I genuinely felt that, as a traditional family shareholder, he had as much right as I had to be a director.

But the point of the EGM was to resolve, one way or another, the split on the Board.

On 27 March 1992, to reassure Celtic supporters in the run-up to the EGM, we announced that Celtic would make an outline planning application for a new stadium on 14 April. Farrell, in a letter to shareholders, immediately condemned Cambuslang on financial, technical and planning grounds – an interesting contrast to his blind faith in Robroyston.

The same day, Fergus McCann entered stage left, denying any involvement with Dempsey or Low or fellow-Canadian Doherty – or anyone. He had formed Celtic's Future plc to raise £17.28 million. McCann would put in £7.2 million. He would raise £5.04 million from a group of unidentified lead investors, and another £5.04 million from fans. He would hold 51% of the shares for five years, and then sell them on to other shareholders (i.e. get his money back). The proposal was conditional on the fans' participation. It was an offer which differed very little from what had been rejected by the Celtic Board a year before I had been co-opted. McCann was certainly consistent in what he wanted, and the same principles appear more or less in the same form in all of his offers.

David was also looking for a way to use the pending EGM productively. And he took the discussion with Gilda and Grant forward at the game the Saturday before the meeting. What David was seeking was a solution that would take the issue of the control of the Club off the agenda, because that was what this was about – not the good of the Club, but the blind determination of a few people to seize control of Celtic.

On the eve of the EGM, Dempsey confirmed this analysis by promising that the battle for control would go on no matter what the outcome. This spelt out what we had suspected all along, that Dempsey was involved in a long-term plan to seize control, and that the saving of Grant and Farrell was merely a skirmish.

The solution David devised was intended to end this guerrilla warfare and to establish long-term peace. He proposed that we draw up a shareholders' agreement which Grant, Kevin, Chris and I would join, pledging each other mutual support. Grant, David, Chris and I pored over the details of this the Sunday before the EGM. Grant was given a copy and went off to seek advice on it. As well as a solution to his own problems, he was also concerned not to abandon Farrell, with whom he had been working closely since we called the EGM. So David drew up a list of rights and privileges that every retired Celtic director would get, which, he said, would allow Farrell to retire with dignity. It wasn't one of his better ideas. Farrell was insulted and enraged when Brian Gilda arranged for the plan to be presented to him. But his friends kept trying to save him, and somehow I found myself leaving Celtic Park at eleven o'clock on the Monday of the EGM to go into town with Grant and David to meet Dempsey, Farrell, Len Murray, and Brendan Somers of the Allied Irish Bank.

I am still not clear exactly what the real purpose of the meeting was. It has been portrayed by Low as our reaction to the granting of the interim interdict knocking out the votes of the partly-paid shares, which Low claims we knew about on the Sunday. The truth is that the writ was not served until the Monday. So neither this meeting nor, more importantly, the shareholders' agreement was a response to a fear of defeat. We believed we would win, but we wanted to end the in-fighting permanently.

In any event, what was discussed at the meeting was our abandoning the EGM. We refused and David began to explain how, if Farrell agreed to retire rather than face the vote, he would still be entitled to his Saturday seat in the box, an invitation to at least one away European tie a year and an allocation of tickets. (And, I thought to myself, David's going to go on and offer him a pie at half-time and a message on the scoreboard on his birthday.) But none of this went down at all well with the comrades.

In the course of the conversation something else emerged which amused David. We had assumed that Brian Gilda was operating on behalf of both Farrell and Grant. But Farrell kept asking 'Who is this Brian Gilda you keep getting to phone me? I know nothing about him at all. What's his angle?'

Then Len Murray mentioned in an affectedly casual way that, of course, we had seen the interim interdict, hadn't we? As they had arranged for it to be served after we had left home for work, and as David's home is in London, naturally we hadn't. I asked for a copy, which appeared to surprise him – much too direct. But he handed one over and it was studied in the car on the way back to the Park. Basically, it interdicted certain of our supporters who held partly-paid shares from voting on the grounds that the transfers were carried out on the wrong forms. Because Chris White had entered a caveat, and would thus have been immediately informed of any interdict, they did not seek one against him. However, the shares were added up wrongly and we took the decision to disallow votes on all of the partly-paid shares. This ruled out a large number of Chris's shares and meant that we lost the vote on Farrell's removal from the Board.

Back at the Park, David, Chris, Kevin, Grant and I had a long and confused meeting over how we could use the EGM to end the hostilities and divisions. All of us tried to persuade Grant to sign the shareholders' agreement. But he was having a real crisis of conscience about it. He believed in the need for change, he wanted to see more money put into the Club. He was even willing to share control, as if being in charge wasn't like being pregnant – you either are or you aren't. He was also concerned about letting the rebel group down and of being seen to 'jump the dyke'. He vacillated for over an hour.

At five-to-two, I cleared the others out of the room and spoke directly to Grant. I told him that I believed that the shareholders' agreement was the way to end the feuding and that he should sign it. But I also told him that whether he signed it or not, I would not vote against him that afternoon. I told him what I genuinely believed, that he had a right to be on the Board, and if all the talk about a family Club meant anything, it meant that I could not vote against another family member. In terms of being a Celtic supporter, I felt closer to Grant than to many of the other directors, and I think that this came across in our conversation. Anyway, he was convinced and at one minute past two he signed and we went upstairs to start the meeting late.

David's co-option to the Board was approved with the support of Grant. The motion against Grant was removed from the agenda. Grant, by agreement, voted for Farrell, who won. So in terms of personalities, it was the status quo; but the signing of the shareholders' agreement ensured a period of stability for a time. The tactic of calling the EGM to concentrate minds had succeeded, and we were quite happy that Farrell had survived, because we were not out for blood. Indeed, as soon as the result was declared I went over and shook his hand. He appeared affected by the gesture and acknowledged his appreciation publicly. I thought we had gone a long way to healing the rift.

I think I was wrong.

Chapter Eight

... Long is the way
And hard, that out of hell leads up to light.

Paradise Lost, 1.432

The shareholders' agreement dealt effectively with the takeover tactics of the rebels. They had run around the shareholders snapping up their holdings or votes, they had threatened and mounted legal challenges, they had spent a lot of money. But we had slammed the door firmly in their faces and had locked a large amount of their money into a hopeless minority position. Dempsey eventually recognised this by unloading most of the shares Low had painstakingly acquired for him to Gerald Weisfeld (many at a loss).

The shareholders' agreement had been entered into because all of the signatories had wanted to commit themselves to working together to solve the Club's problems while being true to its traditions. We were joined by a small band of supporters, our families and friends among the shareholders, who shared our beliefs and who saw the rebels as a bunch of self-seekers whom they would not tolerate at any price (at that time £300 per share) to be involved in the running of Celtic. Our supporters were people who, while concerned that the Club quickly achieve success on the field, were prepared to look beyond current results to what the Club in essence meant and how best to conserve it.

For the four of us (David always insisted that he would go along with what we wanted) it was a recognition that we wanted to work together, and also that we recognised the high price that our shares commanded depended on their control value. By binding together we were indicating that we were prepared to forego the realisation of that value for the sake of the Club.

It was a big sacrifice for Chris, particularly, but also for Grant

102

and Kevin. It was less so for me, although I was the only one who had actually bought shares. One particular purchase was critical in denying the rebels the 50% they thought they were about to achieve. These were Paul Fitzpatrick's. He was a school friend of my cousin David, and David told Paul that if he decided to sell and reached agreement on price he should sell to me. He did, and the day after he phoned, my wife Zita flew down to London to complete the deal. Even this was carried out in the midst of much soul-searching by Chris. It was only after Dempsey, at Easter Road, congratulated me on securing them that I realised just how critical they were.

At any rate, we had settled the control argument and had rendered the rebels' plotting and scurrying about and their insidious media campaign futile. We could now concentrate on addressing the real problems that faced the Club. Certainly David, Chris and I had a clear idea of what those problems were and of their scale. This was not just a matter of getting a winning team, although that would have been the biggest single factor in relieving the PR pressure. It was obvious that football had changed. The factors causing that change were still at work – and against clubs playing in as small a country as Scotland.

Clubs were increasingly dependent on non-gate income: that means sponsorship and advertising; that means audience and exposure; that means television – and television wants those games which attract the biggest audiences. In a country with a population of only five million, the television audience, the returns from advertisers (and therefore the fees) were inevitably smaller. And whereas English televised football is exportable, Scottish football, in general, is not. So there was – and is – no possiblity that money that would have to be sunk into revitalising Celtic Park would be recouped from any future income flows which even a successful Celtic could generate. If in addition you were unwilling to allow a rich individual to sink his money into the bottomless pit of a football club's bank account, as we were, then you had to devise another method for raising the capital.

It was as a direct result of studying these realities that we came so strongly to favour Cambuslang. The Cambuslang option would not only have provided Celtic with a new, modern stadium but also with a flow of income from the profits of that asset. This 'new money' would be poured every year into strengthening the team. It was the solution that would provide the financial answer, while allowing the traditional values of the Club to be preserved. Before that solution could be achieved, however, funding had to be secured for what was a large and ambitious project. This was a difficult and tortuous process, with many false dawns, and our efforts to achieve the right funding package drove us to the conclusion that control must eventually pass from the families; but we were determined that this should not simply be to a faction, a new dynasty. The eventual plan announced by David in February 1994 brilliantly solved all these problems, and would have taken the Club beyond family and faction. I believe that that was also why our solution was so mercilessly attacked by our opponents – even though it closely resembled Dempsey's Robroyston scheme. The big difference was that we had worked out how Cambuslang was to be funded. The funding for Robroyston, we had been told, would look after itself. Which was the greater 'pie in the sky'?

Though drafts of Gwyn Kennedy's investigations of potential stadium sites had been much leaked to the Press, for them to dismiss, the final document which landed on the directors' desks at the end of 1992 was quite straightforward. Fifteen sites had been looked at, including Robroyston and Celtic Park itself. In most cases, there were major infrastructure defects, such as fragmented land ownership or transportation deficiencies. Robroyston was located near a motorway but was in the greenbelt, with years of delay in overcoming the wishes of a reluctant planning authority, Glasgow District Council.

The site at Cambuslang offered by far the best prospect. It was, essentially, a brownfield site (though nothing had ever been built on this particular patch of ground). It was in single ownership – the Glasgow Development Agency – and the owners wanted it developed. As in all parts of the Glasgow area (including Robroyston and Celtic Park), there were mineworkings beneath the surface, but engineers know how to deal with such matters. Surrounding the site to the north and east of the Clyde, and to the west of the soon-to-be-reopened Coatbridge rail link from Rutherglen, were genuine brownfield areas, the remnants of the wreckage of the metal-working industries of the 19th and early 20th centuries.

Here, there was space for everything we needed to make it possible for Celtic, the football club, to survive with its traditions, while its financial needs were met by commercial activities which could co-exist around a magnificent multi-purpose stadium complex. The old thinking that every club needed to own its own ground, which lay unused for thirteen days out of fourteen, could be supplanted by a new vision . . . a leisure and recreation centre in a much-neglected part of Glasgow, where not only football but other sports and also musical and any large-audience events could be staged. It would be a major and permanent new asset for the city, to rank with the triumphs of the Garden Festival and the Year as European City of Culture. It would rival the best of European and world-class facilities – and it would put Ibrox into the shade.

Terry Cassidy had been waiting for the right moment to announce all this. It was immensely exciting news. We all hoped it would prove the catalyst which would turn the public relations battle and bring the fans what they desperately wanted – a forward-looking plan of action for the Club. With the EGM past and the shareholders' agreement in place, Cassidy took the earliest opportunity, the following Wednesday, giving us a bare two working days to get the news conference organised.

But Cassidy himself had a small problem: he was due to catch the morning flight to the USA that day. The news conference would have to be a breakfast one starting at nine o'clock. Mike Stanger was despatched to make the arrangements. For the hacks who were not used to being up and about at this time of the morning, the catering provided included a full Scottish breakfast – and annular doughnuts, shaped like the proposed stadium, topped in green and white hooped icing. There was to be a detailed presentation by the Superstadia team, including Gwyn Kennedy, and the architects, Seiferts. Given the persistent criticism that we never made enough information available, this was to be the exception. Caldwell, in his book, complains there were too many facts!

The news release was explicit, to the point and journalistically correct in containing the summary of the whole within the first two paragraphs:

An application for outline planning permission for a new stadium complex to be built on a 30-hectare site at Cambuslang was submitted to Glasgow District Council before Easter, following positive meetings with the Glasgow Development Agency over the use of the land.

The GDA has given its backing to the scheme and is doing what it can to facilitate it. Meanwhile, the planners have asked the Club to prepare a traffic analysis and an environmental impact study, which is part of the normal process in plans of this magnitude.

The Stadium Plans
The Cambuslang scheme proposed is a careful blend of sporting and commercial developments, each designed to complement the other in terms of the facilities provided and the mutually-supportive funding. The stadium can, of course, exist without the adjoining hotel and other facilities. But, more significantly, they would not be viable without the association with the stadium. The scheme comprises:

- a circular stadium seating 52,000 in two tiers
- a 200-bedroom hotel, linked directly to the stadium
- a Celtic Heritage museum
- integrated leisure and sports facilities within the stadium
- a permanent performance stage
- mobile acoustic curtain enclosing seating areas of 3,500-15,000
- a retail village, including car showrooms
- class 4 office units
- an 8-screen cinema complex
- a 30-lane tenpin bowling alley
- drive-through fast food restaurants
- two park-and-ride railway stations
- parking for more than 4,500 vehicles, including a VIP valet parking area
- a petrol filling station
- room for further expansion

The complete development is valued at £100 million, of which the single biggest element will be the stadium at just under half the total cost.

Importantly for funding credibility, the stadium itself is

capable of being developed in three principal segments. The two 'touchline stands' can be constructed first, to provide seating for 32,000 spectators, at a cost of £26 million. A further 10,000 seats can be provided for just £4 million more, on the lower decks of the two 'end-stands'.

At a later date, if sufficient capital funding is not immediately forthcoming, increased revenues from the stadium operations, including associated commercial developments, will make it possible to complete the upper decks of the end-stands, to provide the final 10,000 seats, at a further cost of £15 million.

A total of 15 sites for a possible new stadium were investigated in detail for us by independent consultants, and Cambuslang was clearly the best – principally because, being a 'brownfield' site, there were unlikely to be insuperable difficulties in obtaining planning permission for the full package of proposals.

The Funding Equation

What is proposed, and what has been discussed in positive terms with the planners, is a practical and versatile stadium complex which is economically self-sustaining. Football will be at the centre of activity, but it will have an economic life of its own beyond Saturday afternoons.

The funding package needed to enable the development to take place will now be progressed in the expectation that planning permission will be forthcoming in the next couple of months.

The funding equation for the development is expected to be made up in a variety of ways: development land sales, the Football Trust, preferential seating bonds, box sales, capital allowance, sponsorship, and public sector grants.

These will all help to fund the stadium itself, and the mix will depend on how we get on with our negotiations and commercial offers. The various supporting developments will be funded by those interested in operating them, not by the club.

To enable the development to take place, a separate limited company is likely to be formed to construct and operate the new stadium. The stadium company's share structure and its Board will be determined by funding considerations. Thus, any shareholder who wishes to become involved with this development may be able to do so through the new company.

If outline planning permission is forthcoming at an early date, a detailed application will follow shortly afterwards. It is expected that work can begin this year, with a scheduled completion date (at least for the first phase) in the second half of 1994.

Celtic Chairman Kevin Kelly says: 'Celtic supporters are entitled to a dream. That dream could be in our grasp at Cambuslang, which is so close to our traditional heartland. But we need to pull together and make it happen. Our task is to make sure that all genuine Celtic supporters have a chance to participate in the development in a meaningful manner.

'What we have here is an ambitious proposal which will of itself contribute to the regeneration of the East End of Glasgow. It is right and proper that football should be the catalyst for economic change. It is also appropriate for Celtic to be taking a lead in providing the city with a broad-based and forward-looking sports facility fit for the foreseeable future.'

The Celtic Stadium: Background Material
In May 1991, Celtic Football Club appointed Superstadia Ltd to prepare a feasibility study to examine the stadium options open to the Club under the terms of the Taylor Report, and to recommend a way forward. The study required to be comprehensive, to identify a suitable site and an acceptable stadium format, and to propose a credible funding mechanism.

The first stage of the study examined 15 sites, measuring each against a pre-determined list of criteria: size, ownership, location, access, planning status and so on. Through a process of elimination, three sites were shortlisted and examined in a detailed comparative analysis: Parkhead, Linwood and Cambuslang.

For each option, a development mix was proposed which contained as its focus a multi-role events stadium, capable of hosting a range of sport and entertainment. The format for the stadium remained constant throughout and, in more detail, consisted of:

• a circular stadium in two tiers, of a final capacity of

52,000 spectators, with the capability of being constructed in three phases

- a performance stage, capable of being lowered beneath ground level for advance preparation without disturbing the day-to-day operations of the stadium

- a movable acoustic and heat-insulating curtain which allows the stadium to operate flexibly as an events arena of varying capacity (from 3,500 to 15,000 spectators): when the curtain is dismantled and the stage re-orientated by 180°, the entire stadium can be used as an auditorium

- a structure which is partially roofed, sufficient to cover the seated areas at all times. A final decision on a full roofing system is considered premature, but the structure will be capable of supporting either a fixed or an opening roof system at some time in the future.

- a range of seat type, with premium seating being arranged in the midfield positions: there will be provision for up to 100 executive boxes

- a fully-serviced complex, ranging from restaurants of differing price and type to fast food at concourse level. The operation of the 200-bedroom hotel, linked directly to the structure of the stadium, would mesh with catering for the boxes and other quality restaurants around the stadium

- leisure and sports facilities which will be contained within the main stadium structure

- a Celtic Heritage museum

- opportunities for community facilities to be developed at reduced cost within the stadium superstructure.

The Support Village
The possibility of developing a full support village at Linwood and Parkhead was severely limited: this was one of the principal reasons for favouring the Cambuslang site, with a much reduced contingency plan for remaining at Parkhead. In addition to the stadium features described above, the support village at Cambuslang would include:

- a 200-bedroom hotel with function facilities, integrally linked with the stadium
- 4,500 car parking spaces, including VIP and valet parking areas
- two railway stations for park-and-ride journeys to and from the city
- a support village containing 15 popular shops (newsagent, chemist, bank, etc.)
- fast-food drive-through facilities
- a petrol-filling station
- an 8-screen cinema complex
- a 30-lane tenpin bowling alley
- some car showrooms and other business class buildings

The Community Benefits

The whole development is designed as a 21st-century facility which will enhance Glasgow's drive to promote itself as a modern, international city.

During construction, several hundred jobs will be sustained, and, once in operation, the complex is expected to support several hundred more jobs. It is therefore expected to be a major factor in the regeneration of the economy of the Cambuslang area.

The Superstadia study also considered the potential benefits for the area around the present stadium which might be stimulated by the relocation to Cambuslang: further work on progressing some of these ideas and opportunities is anticipated.

The Next Steps

The Superstadia feasibility study was presented to the Celtic Board in January 1992. As this project will be one of the most fundamental and formative in the history of the Club, it was important for the Board to consider the findings of the study in a balanced and business-like manner. Projects of this size and complexity would tax even the largest company.

Before a decision to apply for planning permission was made, the consultants were asked to develop some of their concepts further, to review others and, along with the Club, to consult key public sector bodies and seek their support.

This has now been done, and the Board feels confident

enough to proceed with the planning application and thereby to declare their intention to relocate to a new stadium at Cambuslang. So what happens next?

• The planning application now enables further negotiations and planning on funding issues to be progressed.

• The successful granting of planning consent will enable the Board to make a final decision on the move to Cambuslang.

• The progress of the fund-raising activities will enable a decision to be made on the phasing of the development.

• All these factors will determine the nature of the corporate structure to be put into place to enable the development to proceed.

• A start on construction can be made before the end of 1992.

• The stadium is scheduled to open for business in the second half of 1994.

The journalists who attended sat in rapt attention as the details were spelled out. Among their considerable number were all the principal business journalists, the television and radio news reporters, and a few (but by no means all) sports reporters. They complained about the early hour of the news conference. Six months later, when more details of the scheme were given at an early afternoon news conference, there was only one sports reporter present – Jim Black of the *Sun* ('Slim Jim', as Cassidy dubbed him, a name he proudly displayed on his column the day after!). Incredibly, all the others gave the occasion a miss – because there was an Under-21 International at Fir Park that afternoon. And, although details of the innovative way in which the proposals would be funded was described with some candour by Patrick Nally, those sports hacks who were absent were always able to claim that Celtic had never explained fully how the stadium would be funded. There are none so deaf as those who will not turn up to be told, none so blind as those who will not see only one point of view.

Nally explained that the funding approach was based on the capitalisation of the marketing rights which the stadium would generate once constructed. He told the news conference that he

111

had identified between fifteen and twenty different product lines and services, the suppliers of which he expected to be interested in having exclusive commercial access to the stadium development. The obvious example is the sale of soft drinks: knowing the capacity of the stadium and the number and type of events planned, it was possible to predict the aggregate audience in a typical year. From that, an interested company could estimate the number of soft drinks which would be sold and therefore the profit generated. A ten-year profit estimate would be made, and the exclusive soft drink rights for that period would be sold for an up-front capital sum.

Nally also mentioned other product lines – obvious ones, such as photographic film, confectionery, fast food and leisure clothing; and less obvious ones, such as telephones, electrical power supply and computer equipment. Each one would contribute towards the total, which Nally estimated as up to £20 million, and this would be part of the construction funding. Nally also indicated that the Cambuslang stadium was just one of a chain of linked stadia to facilitate the planning of major concert tours by big-audience musical stars and other entertainers. The commercial rights would, of course, only have a value once the stadium had been constructed; however, Nally was convinced that the idea was bankable. In other words, a merchant bank would, for a fee, be prepared to underwrite a major part of the initial construction costs – and that's the £20 million that Gefinor, a Swiss merchant bank, eventually agreed to put up as part of a wider package for the proposed network of stadia.

Meanwhile, following our demonstration of unequivocal control at the end of April 1992, McCann for the second time withdrew his offer to finance a takeover of Celtic. We were glad to see him lift that particular proposal from the table, but we were sorry to see him walk off in the huff. If only he could have been convinced of the viability of Cambuslang, he could have played a major role in it – and saved himself the money I think he is going to lose in Celtic.

The rebels, on the other hand, were glad to see the back of him, I suspect. Dempsey and the others who had told McCann before the EGM that they were eager to join his group of 'lead investors' to put up £5 million, had withdrawn their commitment and McCann left in disgust. The problem that the rebels had with McCann was that he did actually have the amounts of money needed to deliver on his rhetoric. To those in Scotland who would have had to scrape together the grub-stake to stay with him, but only in a minority position, his approach was to be discouraged rather than supported. It was control that they wanted, and for themselves. They were right to fear his financial power – as the make-up of the new board demonstrates. When I met McCann in Montreal later that year, he confirmed that their failure to produce the promised money had led to his retreating back to Canada.

Three weeks later, the rebels were said to be meeting in Bermuda for what was reported as 'a council of war' – more like a holiday, I thought. A week later, Low sent me a cutting about David. It was about the Gateway takeover, for which David had been widely praised, but this particular newspaper item criticised him. Low, ever the pragmatist, was always prepared to enter into discussions with me and to make it clear that we could be allies rather than enemies any time I wanted.

By early June 1992, the Bermuda pact surfaced, with Doherty and twelve others requisitioning another EGM. This was to consider their proposal to increase the Club's share capital to £84,500 by the issue of 29,500 new ordinary shares and the 30,000 'deferred' shares, to be purchased for £75 each by Dempsey and Eddie Keane. Existing shareholders would be invited to subscribe for new ordinary shares at £75. Their requisition for the EGM was incorrectly drafted, and had to be lodged again eleven days later. So much for 'The Bungling Board'!

On BBC Radio Scotland, Dempsey submitted himself to questioning. The interviewer was perceptive: 'Is this scheme not simply to secure the backing of smaller shareholders?' 'We haven't spoken to any' was the answer Dempsey gave, to disguise the fact that his spending frenzy had removed many of the original small shareholders. 'Is this all about Celtic Football Club, or is it about yourself and others wanting to take control?' asked the interviewer. 'This does not make provision to take control, it's quite unfair and hypocritical in the extreme to suggest that,' replied Dempsey. In fact, we now know from Low's account that Dempsey and Low were meeting twice a week to plan the takeover of the Club, and were in the middle of scooping up as many shares as they could.

Three days later, more hypocrisy, more sophistry. At a rally of the Affiliation of Registered Celtic Supporters' Clubs, called to consider a possible boycott, Dempsey said guardedly: 'I've done it. I've cancelled executive boxes, advertising and match sponsorship.' Later, he denied inciting fans: 'You can't lead people into a boycott, they have to make up their own minds. Changes at clubs come about when fans vote with their feet. Absence of support and paying customers forces boardroom changes.'

A week elapsed. Through the intermediation of Brian Gilda of Peoples, Kevin and I met Dempsey to discuss an end to the hostilities. It was a most peculiar meeting. I was there to explore what exactly Dempsey was looking for. If it was reasonable, an accommodation might have been reached. 'I don't want anything,' he kept insisting, until Len Murray intervened to point out the obvious. 'I think that you will gather from what Brian says that he does not want anything from you or from Celtic.'

But something was troubling Dempsey. He had purchased a large number of shares which were unregistered by the Board. One part of a solution which Brian Gilda advanced was that Dempsey should dispose of a large proportion of the shares in return for the remainder of, say, one thousand being registered. Another suggestion was that Dempsey would authorise Brian Gilda to represent his interest in his Celtic shares and Gilda would go on the Board. Although letters were drafted to this effect, the idea was taken no further.

Eventually, Dempsey announced a year-long moratorium during which he would not support calls for another EGM. He had recognised that the shareholders' agreement had deprived him of the fire-power to win. He had apparently also instructed Low 'to concentrate on buying more shares'.

I got the impression at the time that Dempsey was torn in two. One part of him wanted to give up the whole struggle. The other wanted to hang on, without any clear plan, to see what developed that he could exploit to the Board's detriment.

Within three weeks, the 'peace' was prejudiced by another piece of mischievous disinformation to the Press, this time the *Sunday Mirror* (the rebels certainly knew how to spread their favours around): 'If the Club is not on a firm financial footing inside six months, the Board would be prepared to step aside.' A spokesman for the rebels was quoted. No confirmation was sought from the Board.

A full six weeks went by with nothing in the Press. Then

there appeared a big effort to discredit the Cambuslang site by anticipating insuperable environmental problems in its development. Strangely, the *Herald* (by now it had dropped its titular attachment to Glasgow) put a ludicrous story obtained from a fanzine on its front page: 'Toxic timebomb . . . methane cloud 4½ miles long could ignite and incinerate the local population . . .' and other such ridiculous claims. I pointed out to the *Herald* correspondent that methane was lighter than air and invisible, thus explaining methane clouds was as challenging to physicists as were black holes.

As soon as we could arrange it, David and I travelled to Montreal to try to persuade Fergus that the proper way to help the Club was to become involved in the financing of Cambuslang. The meeting was not a success. As we sat down in the office of his financial adviser, Fergus's first words to me, after I had asked him to support us, were: 'Have you got £5 million to put up? No? Well, come back when you have.' He was ready to end the meeting there and then, but his colleague kept it going for David to explain our case in detail. But he wasn't interested. He wasn't even interested in being hospitable, he just wanted us out and did not give himself the chance to get to know us or make an assessment of us for himself.

I was also trying to make up my mind about him. I had gone to discover whether Fergus was actually the person to entrust with transforming the Club. He convinced me that he was not. Further, I concluded that if he were to be allowed to put money up in the way that he wanted to, he would simply lose it. I came to this conclusion not eagerly but sadly, because with all of the busted flushes in Glasgow claiming the right to put money in, I never at any time doubted that Fergus both had the finance and was willing to plough it in to Celtic. When I flew out of Montreal the next day I was convinced that to invite him in would be detrimental to Celtic. And not too clever for him, either. Now that he is in charge, I will have the chance to see how accurate my judgment was.

At the end of the 1992-93 season, the Board sat down with Liam ready to review another barren season. The manager argued that new players were needed, and after discussion with the bank Chris reported that we could raise the overdraft further to make £2 million available to him. I was resolutely opposed to giving him any money at all. He had promised, in his job interview and afterwards, to win a trophy in his first season – that was the management goal that we agreed with him and he had not come remotely near doing that. Indeed, the results in the Skol and Scottish Cups suggested that he had not appreciated exactly what was required of a Celtic manager.

I found this difficult to explain. On a personal basis, I liked Liam. He was intelligent and possessed a cosmopolitan outlook, though basically shy and therefore difficult to get to know. He always thought before he spoke, which gave him authority his youth might otherwise have undermined. Brady had been a winner with Arsenal and in Italy, but he never conveyed to me that he had brought the necessary determination and urgency to the Celtic job. Perhaps after the heights he scaled at Wembley and in the most difficult league in the world, he found the Scottish scene a bit Mickey Mouse.

Anyway, I did not feel that the reward for a season of failure was to throw money at the manager, especially when he had proved himself an indifferent trader. Cascarino had been a disaster. And Gillespie and Mowbray hardly inspirational. I felt there was nothing to suggest that he would spend an extra tranche of money wisely. And it seemed to me that pushing the overdraft up still further was hardly a sensible thing to do. I was out-voted six-to-one and Brady bought Stuart Slater and Andy Payton.

The decision to release the money was done, as it always was, in consultation with the manager but with no discussion at all about the players that might be bought. That decision was entirely the manager's. When Brady announced that he was going for Slater, I had grave doubts. All I knew about him was that he had scored only one goal for West Ham the previous season. That was enough. Slater's subsequent career suggests that I was right. Brady also (on and off) talked about buying Robert Fleck. Grant and I both warned him of the consequences of that! But he was not deterred, and if the player's price had fallen he would have brought him to Celtic Park. Again, Fleck's failure to make much impact after his transfer to Chelsea suggests that he too would have been a flop.

A new season always brings fresh hope, especially with another couple of million to spend on players. For the fans, they can put behind them the disappointments of the last year on the field. For Celtic, though, and for Liam Brady in particular, it was vital that the team got off to a winning start. We had just managed

116

to squeeze into Europe, by default, and it would be great if we could set up our season with a good run there. Apart from the unbudgeted funds which it would bring in, the fans would be happy and the rebels would be kept quiet.

So the first round tie with Cologne was vital. Everyone in the Club looked forward to European trips, with the excitement of air travel, the luxury of five-star hotels and the spending money. When I joined the Board Celtic followed the SFA tradition of giving each member of the party, including directors, a *per diem* allowance. I thought it was pathetic and advised Chris to stop it, which he did: from then on, only incurred expenses were reimbursible against receipts.

I also found these trips tedious. I had better ways to spend my time than lounging about in hotels in provincial towns for three or four days. It's fine for the players and coaching staff – they are working – but the directors sit around for half a week with nothing to do except fill in the time until kick-off. So I tended to fly out on the day of the game and come back on the plane with the team.

When I arrived in Cologne on the afternoon of the game I was the last of several thousand supporters. I walked from the station with David, absorbing the atmosphere. Down a side-street, I spotted a mobile sculpture which I immediately recognised as a Rickey. Rickey was an American sculptor whose work was very popular, and whose father had been general manager at Singer's in Clydebank. Rickey's work combined the metal-working skills of Clydeside with art. But the SECC had turned down an opportunity to have a specially commissioned Rickey outside their door: instead, they've got a miserably prosaic illuminated logo. David was amazed by this off-the-cuff information from his companion, but he didn't know I was Patron of the Scottish Sculpture Trust and had met Rickey in Glasgow the year before.

For the first time, the presence of so many supporters together worried me. Most of them had had a lot to drink and they were carrying extra rations with them. Although they were friendly to me and to the local population as we walked through them on the way from the Cathedral, I realised how easy it would be for trouble to be triggered off. I also saw them, for the first time, through the eyes of the German businessmen and shoppers. I was embarrassed for Celtic. I was also worried that we were walking a tightrope as far as their behaviour is concerned. Neither Celtic nor Scotland fans have got into trouble recently, but really the mixture is so volatile that the least little incident could trigger off a major problem.

Coincidentally, we were drawn against another German team in the next round, Borussia Dortmund. That was when Liam went into a deep huff with me. Fed up with hanging around the hotel in Essen on the afternoon of the game, I commandeered the team bus to take me, my wife Zita, Tom and Angela Grant, Kevin and one or two others into Dortmund to attend an open-air function that the town had organised for the fans.

As we headed back into Essen, I noticed that the driver was taking a somewhat circuitous route back to the hotel. I could not get much sense out of him because of his language problem (he couldn't speak English), so told him to stop at a policeman on points duty. He was able to tell me that an unexploded bomb had been discovered by builders on a site near the hotel and that traffic had been banned from the area. I tried to explain that we were Celtic directors who had to get the team bus back to the hotel so it could take the team to the game. Now, the German education system is good, but you can hardly expect it to teach a traffic cop the vocabulary to deal with this. He did laugh, however, when I asked him of the bomb: 'Is it one of ours?' We eventually had to abandon the bus and, with the help of a police lieutenant whose flexible attitude contradicted every stereotype of Germans-in-authority, I got a police car through to the hotel, where I guided the team – kit, cases and all – to the safe area where the bus was parked. Liam was not amused.

Brady might have laughed if he had been at the pre-match dinner the previous evening. As usual, this took place in the private room of an elegant restaurant where pleasantries and gifts were exchanged between the clubs. Generally these gatherings were stupefyingly boring, with language barriers stifling any conversation. This one was dragging on even longer than normal so I stood to make an impromptu farewell speech. I finished by announcing the end of the function so that the Germans could get to the stadium and put their towels on the seats!

After our victory over the two legs, things were quiet in the Press, demonstrating again that much of the 'bad PR' which the Club suffered over this period directly reflected the fortunes of the team on the field. If we'd had success there, the Press would have been unable to criticise the Board so stridently and the rebels would not have found fertile ground in which to sow the seeds of discontent. We would have had time and space to effect our plans.

On 2 October 1992, *Scotsport Extra Time* produced a story which damaged the Board's credibility. It was announced that Laing Construction had made 'an amazing offer' of £50 million to re-build and re-develop Celtic Park. The impression was built up that this was a gift, a quite extraordinary and unrepeatable one: '£50 million will not be offered again'. It was only towards the end of the item that it was hinted that what was involved was 'a mortgage-like arrangement', i.e. a loan, with all the financial burdens this would entail. (The Board had, of course, been frequently criticised for running up ever-greater debts.) But the most damaging assertion was that Laing's offer would be withdrawn if it wasn't accepted within the week-long deadline the company had supposedly set the Board. Now, of course, an international company of the standing of Laing had made no such threat, and no such offer, as the company itself stated unequivocally in a news release the following week:

> Laing Scotland approached Celtic Football Club several weeks ago concerning the possible construction of a new stadium or the renovation of Celtic Park. At no time was any offer of financial assistance made and, therefore, there was no deadline to be met. The talks with Celtic were constructive and we have taken up the Club's suggestion and contacted the Superstadia consortium. We are also working on some of our own ideas to present to Celtic in the future. At this stage, it is too early for any further comment.

Scottish Television never referred to Laing's rebuttal.

Ten days later, the Glasgow Development Agency gave Celtic a two-year option to purchase the 33-hectare site at Cambuslang at a price of £2 million. This was the first of three stages in the assembling of the Cambuslang package – the other two being the gaining of planning permission and the securing of the finance.

Cassidy went off on three weeks' holiday. While he was away, members of the Board pondered his future. Farrell and Grant hadn't voted for him when he was first appointed. External opinion, no doubt whipped up whenever it suited the rebels, had turned vehemently against him. But all of that was of no importance whatever. The only thing that mattered was whether he had done what he had been hired to do, namely to progress a solution to the stadium problem and to develop commercial activities to put the Club on a surer financial footing. Without doubt he had made progress on the stadium, but much slower than we would have liked. On the financial side, he had warned us publicly that it would take two years before any benefits were discernible, and this was just twenty-two months into his three-year contract. Nevertheless, in the Board's view most of his commercial initiatives had given us no signs of success, despite major expenditure on staff and other resources. 'The Family Club' was a spectacular failure. The shops were not making much progress. The real success had been the Umbro kit deal. The 1991-92 accounts were about to be published, showing a pre-tax loss of £3.2 million. The Press – and some sponsors – were disenchanted with him.

We decided to dispense with his services.

Cassidy returned from his holiday on Saturday 24 October 1992. Chris was to phone him at home and ask him to come in to meet us. His plane was significantly delayed but we wanted the matter dealt with immediately to prevent rumours and leaks. Chris kept phoning and eventually got an answer. Cassidy, jet-lagged, was understandably reluctant to come in; but he eventually did so and was given the news after the game. It has been written that I was the director who summoned Cassidy to that meeting. Of course I wasn't – that was not my job, because I was a non-executive director.

The rebels were gleeful. The *Daily Record* ran a totally inaccurate story that directors were considering giving personal guarantees to the bank. And the whole cycle of misery was given a further twist. It enabled the rebels to emerge again, just five months into the 'year of peace' which Dempsey had promised Kevin. Now they promised a new power bid at the Club's forthcoming AGM.

The rebels' attempts to involve the Bank of Scotland continued with a 'warning' from Doherty that the bank were 'very anxious' and might move in first.

To try to allay the possible fears of anyone in public or business life who might by now have some reason to believe Celtic's directors had completely lost the place, we decided to appoint Ernst & Young, a major international firm of professional advisers, as our project manager for the Cambuslang stadium. Such a firm always does a detailed and exhaustive 'position audit' before taking on projects, and we were confident that they would find that the elements of the Cambuslang scheme stacked up favourably compared with similar property-based development projects. And so it proved.

To tackle the daily management problems David set up simple and effective systems of control. His success in ensuring that the business side of Celtic was run very tightly is demonstrated by the fact that McCann's 'independent' audit failed to discover the black hole that was said to exist in the accounts. The Club refused to make a copy of this report available to me on the grounds that it was prepared 'for internal purposes only'. McCann complains about the treatment of Cambuslang which, at the time, was an on-going project. Some £430,000 was spent on development costs. Under Celtic's agreement with Stadivarious this money was recoverable once Cambuslang got under way. It was therefore treated in the accounts as a receivable. Not only was this correct, in addition, the way in which it was treated was highlighted in the accounts and the matter explained at the AGM. It was actions taken after the Board changes which rendered it irrecoverable.

The other allegation that is made is that the overdraft was under-stated by £611,000. It was not. The cash position was treated in the accounts exactly as it had been treated traditionally and the auditors confirm that this was in accordance with the Club's normal practice which was to show the cash book position. The £611,000 relates to three cheques dated 30 June 1993 (the last day of the company's financial year) which had been received by the Club but were not through the bank. What McCann fails to say is that in so far as this money represented prepayments, the liabilities were correspondingly increased so that at no time were they understated.

Mind you, David could not always control every penny that was spent. Hardly was Cassidy out the door when Grant was visited by a photocopier salesman, and on the basis of a promise of sponsorship he signed a deal which committed the Club to over £120,000 on office equipment. He was misguided enough to believe that the deal was going to cost us less than our existing arrangement. Try as Chris did to get us out of the deal, he found that a legally-binding contract had been signed by Grant before he ran to Chris with the problem. So Chris could only reduce our liablity marginally. And we had redundant photocopying machines falling out of ever cupboard! The promised sponsorship never materialised.

Then, out of the blue, Cassidy sent in the Sheriff Officers on a Mickey Mouse mission to poind the Club's principal asset, the stadium, against his claim for compensation on his dismissal.

All the while, lawyers were working for the rebels, to try to find illegality in the shareholders' agreement. Low had a wheeze about Celtic being subject to the rules of the Takeover Panel (the Stock Exchange's watchdog body to ensure fair play in the conduct of PLC takeovers). He asked that august body for a ruling, to which McNee duly gave grave and serious prominence on *Scotsport Extra Time*. So did Kevin McCarra in *Scotland on Sunday*: 'The move will impair the Board's ability to block attempts by dissident shareholders to win control, and casts a shadow over the Cambuslang stadium project.' He didn't explain how.

Two weeks later, our solicitors advised us of the Takeover Panel's entirely predictable verdict: 'The Panel Executive concluded the Celtic company had a totally private feel and should not come under the Code . . . In particular the reference to the terms of the Celtic Articles of Association which gave the Celtic Board the final say as to the registration of a transfer or the refusal to register had been conclusive.' The Takeover Panel went on to express its displeasure that a confidential referral had been leaked to the Press.

Another waste of Celtic time and money.

But the rebels didn't care whether they were right or wrong. The shareholders' agreement had effectively stymied their plan to grab control, and they were now damaging Celtic by setting us off on expensive wild goose chases and by demeaning the Club in the eyes of the support and the public. Stability was their enemy, so they set out to de-stabilise.

Casting around desperately for some way to inject a better atmosphere into everything surrounding Celtic, I made a major mistake. David wanted us to appeal to the natural good humour of the fans. The Celtic fanzines had built up quite a following and, although the other directors said they never read them, I did and so did David. We were greatly amused by their inventiveness and (until more recently) lack of malice. David thought we should turn the tables on the Press and have a feature in *Celtic View* which cast a sardonic eye on the hacks and their ways in exactly the same way as the fanzines did the Board.

David asked me to pursue the idea. Of the two fanzines, we both thought *Once a Tim* had the better cutting edge. It was crueller. So I invited its editor, Matt McGlone, to meet me in my office. We exchanged pleasantries, as one does on first meeting someone, and I answered every question he had about the current situation, assuming him to be a genuine Celtic supporter. He was particularly anxious to know whether or not David was a mason! 'How could I know?' I asked. 'Wouldn't it be a secret if he were?'

McGlone and I must have talked for an hour and a half, during which time I put my idea to him. Secretly, he was taping the conversation, and later copies found their way to, probably among others, Gerry McNee and the *Evening Times*. It was quite clear from that conversation exactly what I was looking for – a *Private Eye*-type piece on the media which would be published in the Christmas edition of the *Celtic View*. But for the *Evening Times* it became another lucrative one-day sensation: 'Celtic Plot to Smear the Times' screamed the billboards. For McNee, it became a weapon he dangled at me through an otherwise meaningless reference in his column in the *Scottish Daily Express*. In case I'd missed it, he also rang me up and quoted juicy pieces from the tape, 'which I have here in my drawer'. I felt extremely threatened. There is now talk of Celtic involving the same McGlone in representing Celtic fans.

It was a constant factor in the struggle for Celtic's soul that the rebels saw nothing reprehensible in threatening behaviour, in taping or retailing private conversations. And they thought nothing of copying or leaking confidential memos as they strove to steal the ownership of one of Scotland's great footballing institutions. Yet they were the ones who became regarded as saviours and the salt of the earth.

I still puzzle how this behaviour did not provoke an iota of moral judgment by third parties in the media or elsewhere.

Chapter Nine

On all sides, from innumerable tongues,
A dismal universal hiss, the sound of public scorn . . .

Paradise Lost, 1.506

The rebels had a finely developed sense of the dramatic. It wasn't long into the new year of 1993 before they concocted another 'secret' summit meeting in an exotic location, this time New York. So much more interesting than New Lanark. 'We had intended waiting until the end of the season,' Dempsey was quoted as saying. 'But things have deteriorated so much, we can't stand by any longer.' The one-year peace promise by now had no semblance of existence, but no one in the media seemed to mind. In the end, of course, the secret meeting took place in Glasgow, where the (interested) media are more accessible.

At this point the rebels espoused the interest of Gerald Weisfeld, the Englishman who with his Scottish wife built up the What Every Woman Wants retail chain, then sold it for a reputed £40 million. 'He is not the first person to have been spurned by Celtic directors,' the rebels told the Press. Weisfeld had previously approached Chris with a view to becoming involved at Board level, but the matter had been dropped after David joined us. Still, that was a good enough excuse for the rebels to try to knit him in to the panoply of those opposed to the Board.

And so their war continued to sap everyone's strength and divert efforts from constructive to destructive ideas. For the rebels, the main pre-occupation was how to lever open the shareholders' pact and its vehicle, David's brilliantly conceived Celtic Nominees Ltd. For the directors, the main hope was that the team would start winning on the park, because we knew that this was the principal concern of supporters at large.

But, then came the disastrous Cup result on 6 February 1993 – defeat at the hands of Falkirk and another season destined to be trophy-free for Celtic. While the gang of rebels sat like a

124

politbureau of protesters in the row in front of the Directors'
Box savouring every moment of our defeat, Brian Dempsey was
at his unctuous best when asked to join Radio Clyde both before
and after the game. Before the game, Archie McPherson and
Hugh Keevins spoke warmly of the millions which Dempsey
was supposed to be prepared to put into the Club. To the
charge that his interventions were creating problems for the
team and the supporters, Dempsey announced: 'If I am in the
slightest doubt that my conduct is in any way damaging them,
I will withdraw.' After the game he went off for 'an informal
little press conference' before returning to the radio to garner
the accolades of the saviour-in-waiting. It was almost like the
events of Palm Sunday. It was certainly a performance of biblical
proportions.

The next day, 7 February 1993, Dempsey was quoted as saying:
'We will go to the Board in the summer and put our cards on the
table. If our bid fails, the Board will never hear from me again.
I will walk away.' Another deadline. Another empty promise.

At the same time, it was revealed in a news release that we
put out that Chris had received an offer from the rebels to buy
his shares at £300 each. Chris had rejected the offer and called
it 'disruptive'.

A *Herald* story on 16 February 1993 was the first to reveal that
£20 million of underwriting for the Cambuslang development
had been agreed with a consortium of European investors. The
paper quoted Patrick Nally, the Superstadia fundraiser. That
consortium was later scared off by the style and tone of the
media coverage of the Celtic affair. They were not to be the last
to be so discouraged. Indeed, according to Lawrence Davis of
Superstadia, the funding negotiations were made more difficult
and took far longer than they otherwise would have by the hostile
Press coverage.

Celtic's directors could do nothing which wasn't instantly
criticised. We had been scorned for not talking to the fans and
to the media, for not telling them what was going on; so when
we decided to do a series of phone-ins on the Celtic Hotline to
do just that without the filtering effect of so-called 'independent
commentators', we were criticised for ripping-off the fans who
would ring in to listen.

Then there occurred another ridiculous incident, which nevertheless revealed Grant as someone who had more frequent

contacts with the Press than he ever admitted to. In the wake of the defeat by Falkirk, I had suggested at a Board meeting that Brady should be asked to report formally to the Board his plans for the future. Directors are not supposed to comment freely on the performance of either the manager or the players, even when they are leaking their own ideas, not someone else's. But on 22 February 1993 the *Herald* carried a story (coming from a director) critical of Brady's performance as manager, and revealing that Brady had been asked for his managerial blueprint. Brady took exception to this in a serious way, and when he found out that it was Grant who had been involved, he intended condemning it at his regular Friday news conference. He phoned me with an hour to go to tell me what he planned to do. I spoke to him and to Grant and told Brady not to do anything until I got to Celtic Park. I sat in Grant's room with the two of them to try to avert the bad publicity that would follow. Grant's views reflected sentiment in the Board, and, while he should not have published them, Brady was wrong to try to embarrass him publicly. But the manager was obsessed with his standing with the players and the Press. Grant then courageously offered to attend the Press conference with Brady and admit to being the mole. It was just more needless bad publicity.

The orgy of media criticism was described to me privately by Roddy Forsyth, the BBC's football correspondent as 'a feeding frenzy'. Everything critical of Celtic that was spoken in a pub was published and assumed to be true. And everything that was published passed into pub folklore to be regurgitated in ever more bizarre rumour and invention. McNee, on 26 February 1993, claimed that Celtic had complained to the SFA about an article by Mark Hateley which had made critical passing reference to the problems at Celtic Park. We hadn't, nor had McNee rung to check.

Then when it was revealed that the Board had refused to allow a share transfer request by Dempsey, McNee used it as the peg for a prediction: 'Well, this is the final battle looming, I don't think there can be any doubt about that . . . It will be all over by June, one way or the other.'

I tried to project some kind of impression of optimism. Mike Stanger, who felt it was time we made some of the running, suggested I put myself again into the lion's den of Scottish Television's *Sport in Question*. It was a torrid affair which earned a considerable post-programme sympathy vote for my 'courage' in facing up to the barrage of critical questioning. I didn't feel courageous. And when I said what I had always genuinely felt, that Billy McNeill's sacking was a great sadness and that there should perhaps be a place for him at Celtic Park, this was presented as a U-turn. The *Daily Record* couldn't cope with the notion you might respect someone that you found it necessary to dismiss.

Also ignored by Scottish Television was the referee's decision in the Old Firm game the previous week to allow play to restart within seconds of the Celtic goal. When play restarted most of the team had not yet completed their celebrations with the fans in the Jungle. Indeed, two of the players were still inside the centre circle when the restart took place, rendering it illegal. The Press were equally unimpressed by our complaint that the excessively quick kick-off had, in the absence of defenders, almost resulted directly in an equaliser by Rangers.

Nobody could conceive that Celtic might have a legitimate case: our paranoia about referees, particularly in Old Firm games, is legendary. Fortunately, a fan had taken a sequence of pictures of the precise moment of the restart. They were published on 7 April 1993 in the *Celtic View*, showing quite clearly that Paul McStay and Peter Grant were still inside the centre circle, walking back into position as the ball was played. Despite the unequivocal evidence, Alan Davidson, in the *Evening Times*, declared 'the game was legitimately restarted'. The SFA later upheld our complaint and brought the case 'to the attention of the refereeing movement in order that there should be no repetition of such a situation'. Scottish Television refused to feature the incident at all, although the fixture was their featured match. Their excuse was that all six of their cameras had missed the incident. But it was also excluded from the post-match studio analysis where the fact that it had happened too quickly for their cameras supported the Celtic case that it was abnormal.

That refereeing decision was bad enough. But probably the worst refereeing performance of the lot was Bobby Davidson's in the 1970 Cup Final. Celtic had a good team at the time, which could normally overcome any little setback. But that day we had three decisions given against us. Aberdeen got a very weak penalty in the first half for hand-ball against Bobby Murdoch. We had a good penalty claim refused after Bobby Lennox had been brought down. And we had a goal chalked off. Not surprisingly we lost, three-one. It was the biggest refereeing controversy of the Jock Stein era.

Bobby Davidson later became a director of Airdrie, and on one visit there when I was a Celtic director I took the opportunity of raising this game with him. Farrell was standing beside me when I brought it up, but when he heard the way the conversation was going he sloped off. First, I asked Davidson in general terms about the game. He said he couldn't remember it! I then went through the various incidents, but I could not jog his memory. I then raised another controversial incident with him from much earlier in his career, when he had disallowed a Rangers 'goal' in a semi-final against Hibs. He could remember that clearly, right down to the Rangers supporter in the Hampden car park who had threatened him. But he still couldn't remember anything about 1970. I then reminded him that he had left West Germany in a huff in 1974. That was when he claimed to have been promised the World Cup Final on a train to Munich, only to have Sir Stanley Rouse reverse it in favour of Englishman Jack Taylor. He remembered that alright. Yet this was the man who expected immediate, uncomplaining compliance with any of his decisions. Rouse had picked Taylor simply because he was English. 'So there was discrimination in football,' I concluded. He stopped talking then.

At the beginning of May 1993, the planning application for Cambuslang was considered by Glasgow District Council's Planning Committee. I attended the hearing, which was held in public. It was pretty dramatic in its own way. The police and Strathclyde Region's roads department voiced objections. The roads people wanted more parking space than the 6,500 proposed. Their little red book told them that you had to have one space for every six spectators. Agreeing on a 'typical' large crowd of 44,000, this meant around 7,400 spaces – but Celtic had suggested only 6,500, which still would have made it the biggest car park in Britain! The police, in their submission, pointed out that, with the 6,500 spaces proposed, the site would be very slow to clear and would cause congestion onto surrounding roads. Their experience of big games at Ibrox and Celtic Park was that the crowds dispersed quickly because of the greater incidence of on-street parking. Councillor Pat Lally, Leader of the Council, in brilliant cross-examinations, placed the statements of the two witnesses in opposite corners and destroyed the arguments of both.

The committee went into private session. After a long period of debate, the decision emerged late in the afternoon. Celtic was given the outline planning permission it had sought, and all of the most burdensome conditions which the Region, the police and the planning officials had sought to impose on the approval had been removed or modified. As is standard practice in such cases, the conditions which remained were to be incorporated into a 'Section 50' agreement. Some of these conditions – for example, satisfying the council with a detailed ground condition and environmental report – were pre-emptive to a start being made on the development. Most, however, were not expected to hold up progress. Indeed, in the construction industry the final signing-off of Section 50 agreements often occurs in the very late stages of completion. Legally, outline planning permission does not exist until the Section 50 agreement is satisfied. For all practical purposes, however, Celtic's Cambuslang stadium project had been given the green light by the planning authority.

Since I had gone through the Cambuslang proposals in detail with Gwyn Kennedy, the planning consultant to Superstadia, I was in no doubt that it would be approved. I could now turn my attention to the funding question. This was something I returned to again and again, with Superstadia and David. From a position of scepticism, I became convinced that the funding proposals were sound and achievable. Not only that, Cambuslang represented the only way out of Celtic's wider dilemma. It would provide a new stadium at virtually no cost to Celtic: that would give us the physical capital asset required to underpin the Club's financial regeneration because, if successful, the stadium would provide the Club with an annual flow of profits from non-football sources.

As David spelt out the implications to me it became increasingly apparent that, to achieve the funding package, which required the participation of financial institutions, the control structure of the Club would have to change. My immediate worry, however, was that the whole project had already dragged on too long; every delay was further threatening its credibility. So, as soon as planning permission was obtained, I insisted that Muir Morrison instruct Patrick Nally to produce the necessary underwriting within three months.

The 1992-93 season had been rounded off by the fans singing

farewell to the Jungle, which we seated in the close season for £400,000, demonstrating how quickly and cheaply temporary improvements could be made. I had never stood in the Jungle and was determined to be there on that last day. But the reception that the fans might give me was the problem. Not that I feared physical attack, but there would be a lot of jeering and the inevitable bad Press coverage.

So, for a laugh, I slipped into the costume of Shere Khan, one of the *Jungle Book* characters there to add atmosphere, and melted into the Jungle as a tiger! When Grant saw the photo he insisted that it was doctored. But that was because he had chickened out of standing there himself for the second half.

The parrot was trouble from the start. I had wanted to introduce a mascot similar to those in America, where every baseball team has one, to amuse the crowd before the game, to do charity visits to hospitals and schools and, generally, to use as a marketing tool. But its imposition by an unpopular Board would produce great customer resistance. So, as part of the Jungle's Last Stand, I ran a fancy dress competition. The fans' favourite was the parrot, and Vincent became the first mascot in Scottish football.

The first problem was to get a decent costume within severe budgetary limitations. There was no way Celtic would pay for a decent one. The first head we ordered was too small and looked like an orphaned budgie or a Sea Devil from *Dr Who* when the girls pranced around my office in it. It didn't look too good on me either. The second head was better and we settled for it. But you couldn't see out of it, so that the parrot wandered around the perimeter of the field bumping into photographers and radio commentators and stewards. And players. They hated Vincent. (Grant kept telling me this, but could never articulate why.) Perhaps they, the stars, felt upstaged. Perhaps they feared the cry 'Bring on the Parrot' when things were going badly for the team. The costume was hot and Vincent was invariably sweaty and smelly as he worked the crowd. But generally the wind was normally strong enough to avoid this turning into a negative selling point.

His first appearance was a near disaster for Kirsten, whom I had sent along as the parrot-minder. She dressed casually in shorts, not realising that football clubs are still funny about women. Kirsten kept getting moved away from the dressing room area where she stood waiting for Vincent. Then he appeared. But he had torn the gusset of his emerald costume and Kirsten had to get down on her hands and knees and pin it up, to tutting disapproval – though not, of course, from Vincent!

Being the Celtic parrot, Vincent could not just turn up and perform. He had opinions. My colleague David Solomons was in charge of parrot affairs and dreaded the Monday morning phone calls when the parrot would come on to suggest an expansion of his role. His first idea was that he needed a tray of sweets, which he could throw into the crowd on his way round, but the police banned his throwing things into the terracing. That didn't deter him. He insisted on handing them out, nearly getting himself lynched in the process and costing us a fortune in lollipops.

I then decided to raise his profile by getting a photo of him visiting McStay in the Bon Secours nursing home. But all Press visits were banned by the Club, and first Jordan and then Brady phoned my office to make sure that we weren't trying to bribe a nun to sneak him in.

Then I sent him along to see off a bus load of supporters to Berne. The usual person didn't turn up and David Solomons, a dignified graduate of Glasgow University, refused to demean himself by dressing up. Eventually the bus driver, who was a Rangers supporter, had to be pressed into service for the photo. He was three sizes too big for the outfit and tore it in seventeen places.

I then took Vincent to Berne, which was a strange trip in more ways than one. While we were there, Chris found himself the beneficiary of one fan's dubious reassurances. Obviously one of the vocal minority who had by this time taken to screaming abuse at the Board at every match, he said he hoped we all understood that, whatever the vulgar ot violent nature of their observations, we should know that 'it's not personal'!

Vincent enjoyed the flight, but Grant hated him so much that he had him kidnapped and left him in the British Embassy. When I got back to Scotland, I phoned the Embassy for news of Vincent. It wasn't the easiest conversation to begin with the charge d'affairs: 'Is the Celtic parrot still there?' But the answer came right away: 'He's sitting opposite me in the Ambassador's chair.' We had to pay to fly Vincent back. Then the costume maker, Ms Bacon, sued me for the price of the first head.

That's when I decided to ground Vincent for good.

Almost as comical as the parrot was the exchange of faxes

that I had with Fergus in June 1993. The first was delivered to me at my office. (The fax didn't come to my home, as Caldwell would have it. Mind you, he also says that I 'eyed it with suspicion'. How does he know that? He couldn't just have made it up, could he?) It was the familiar offer in slightly different dressing. I took it seriously and immediately proposed a meeting. But Fergus wasn't interested in discussions. He wanted acceptance of a proposal that would have given him a 51% holding. He knew that I could not agree to that. The faxes went back and forward with no conclusion. He then published them all, despite my request in my first answer that the exchange be kept confidential.

By the time McCann had faxed me, I had made up my mind that he was someone that I would find it very difficult to work with. I had studied his proposals and, having heard him expound on the thinking behind them, I concluded that his analysis was wrong. For a start, he didn't understand the financial environment in which football was now operating. He did not convince me that his ideas would turn the Club round. I was, therefore, not prepared to hand it over to him because I believed that he would devalue the shares and cost the shareholders money. That is why, from this point on, we insisted that he – or anyone else who wanted to run the Club, for that matter – make an offer for the shares. If the shareholders accepted the offer, McCann could go right ahead and risk his own money. But he wouldn't be risking ours, or theirs.

It would have been impossible to tell him this in a fax – particularly one about to be published. A meeting might have secured an offer, or it might have allowed us to persuade him to invest in Cambuslang, which was still the best way in which he could have helped the Club.

At the end of the season the Board told Brady that it wanted to review the playing side with him. I was in no doubt what I wanted to do. I wanted to sack him. Liam had now had two full seasons and was nowhere near winning a trophy. He had been given two large tranches of money and had failed to strengthen the team. I saw no prospect of his succeeding and felt he should go now to let us start the new season with a different manager.

Brady came to the Board meeting and did not satisfy me that he could deliver the necessary strategy or motivation to bring

132

success. But he presented his plan, which involved a complete clear out of the coaching staff. He had drawn up the simplest of organisation charts to show where the new people would fit in. This bowled everyone over. Kevin and Grant studied it as if it was the first one they had ever seen. I felt that, while he was proposing the most radical solution short of his own resignation, it wasn't enough. Management is about leadership and I was doubtful as to whether changing the whole of the management team under a leader who had been proved wanting could work. If it were to work, it would depend entirely on who his new number two was to be – so I asked him who it was. He told us that, while he had a specific person in mind, he wanted to be allowed not to disclose the name. I told him that I thought it was ridiculous that we were being asked to approve a vital apppointment without knowing who it was to be.

In the private discussion which followed, I proposed his dismissal but did not get a seconder. His little chart had done the trick. I also demanded that we be told who he intended appointing as coach. I was a minority of one. This was the only time I fell out with David, whom I expected to back me.

When, some weeks later, Liam told me that his first choice, Joe Jordan, had accepted, I was very disappointed. This was not the bold step needed. Jordan, like Brady, had played his football abroad and brought the same Italian experience and introverted personality. He could hardly have been said to have been a success at Tynecastle. Brady had also told us that the number two was to be called 'coach'. But Jordan had insisted on being called 'assistant manager' and Brady gave in. Not a great start.

At this time, McCann made his correspondence with me public and withdrew the offer. He then advertised in the papers asking for the fans' support and a pound for a copy of his proposals. Neither of the two 'inside' stories of the coup record how much he was sent.

I went to Italy with David to see the pre-season tour. The gap between Celtic and the Italians was embarrassing. We watched one training session when Nicholas decided to practise his shooting. He took a dozens balls to the edge of the box and tried to curl them in at the far post. It wasn't clear exactly what he was trying to do, but he didn't seem to be making a very good job of it. But I was struck mainly by the disorganised nature of his efforts, so different from the thoughtful application of a golfer, say. As far as I could see, football coaching is still in the Corinthian era.

On our return, I picked up the threads of Cambuslang. As a result of the pressure I continued to exert over the funding, Patrick Nally had written to our consultant, Muir Morrison, at Ernst & Young at the end of July 1993, confirming that 'he had been working on the placement of the £20m sponsorship/marketing guarantee'. He reminded Muir that he had 'always anticipated this guarantee being placed with the selected contractor, once secured, who was prepared to give the necessary commitment for the fixed price design-and-build agreement'. And he pointed out that Higgs & Hill were very much in the frame.

He went on: 'The cornerstone funding, as you call it, is being progressed. As you know, I am working with a group of investors to place the physical bank guarantee through Credit Suisse bank in Zurich. I will attempt to get confirmation as far as I am able . . . by 29 July.' He promised to pursue 'a comfort letter which, in many ways, is all you are going to get from the investors at the moment'. However, in response to an exhortation from Muir for Nally to try to speed things up, Nally was doubtful whether he could have the commitment delivered by 27 August 1993, but thought that September was feasible. He reiterated that the decision had been taken to fund the work from outline to detailed planning, and felt that 'having a commitment from a major contractor in place would have been sufficient to meet the demands of the media for a detailed progress report'.

We had concluded three valuable sponsorship deals for the start of the new season. C R Smith went back on the jerseys, Lex Audi completed a car deal with us and Manulife offered financial services to our fans – deals totalling half a million pounds for the next season. But the eve-of-the-season story in the *Evening Times* was not to be any of these positive moves. Rather it was a prediction that our annual accounts would show total debts of £10 million. The figure was fiction.

The whole saga took a predictable twist in August 1993, with McCann and Dempsey said to be launching a new £20 million bid. Or rather, it wasn't a bid. And McCann wasn't involved. Maybe. At 0720 hrs on 24 August, BBC Radio Scotland broadcast Dempsey confirming the joint approach and assuring us that 'it wasn't a bid to take over anything'. And at 1820 hrs on the same day, Scottish Television reported that 'McCann has expressed his surprise at reports linking him to a coalition of wealthy Celtic supporters intent on mounting a £20 million takeover bid for the Club . . . Fergus McCann told me tonight: "I have not spoken to Brian Dempsey in over a year. I am surprised at these reports. If Mr Dempsey is behind them I find them a strange way for him to do business."'

On 15 September 1993 we were able to announce that the Club was making an operating profit. David's systems and supervision had restored trading balance. Mike Stanger copied the press release to the *Evening Times* with the note, 'No doubt you will do your objective best with these figures.' The plea fell on deaf ears.

A week later, McCann made another offer. Dempsey's contribution had shrunk from the millions suggested at Falkirk to one million pounds.

For some time now I had been considering an invitation from the *Evening Times* to put my point of view. I had kept this on hold, to use it at the most effective time. With our annual accounts about to be published, I prepared an article and told them I wanted it published on the following Thursday. They agreed. On the Wednesday before, they published a rehash of the McCann faxes that he had himself given to the press months earlier. They were produced in such a bold and hostile way that my article planned for the following day would have looked pathetically weak in comparison. I withdrew it – as was, no doubt, intended.

In early October 1993, after defeat at Perth, Liam Brady resigned. I came back on the bus with him. He said very little, but when we got to Celtic Park he asked Kevin to come up to his room and there he told him that he had had enough. So we were landed with the situation I had tried to avoid. We had to find a new manager in the middle of the season, with the team already out of two competitions. Jordan, after agreeing to look after the team on a *pro tem* basis, handed in his resignation the following day because – despite Liam's recommendation – we had not offered him the job right away. No one wanted him to be the next manager. Frank Connor stepped into the breech, and in his short spell led an unbeaten team. When Macari was appointed the only condition that we imposed was that Frank, in acknowledgement of his loyalty, had to be kept on.

135

The intolerance and hostility of the fans had dramatically increased. It really never got to me as long as it was just verbal, but I drew the line at excitable and aggressive people trying to lay their hands on me. At McDiarmid Park, after the game, a fan had tried to attract my attention by persistently shouting first 'Kelly', and then, more cunningly, 'Michael'. I didn't respond to either, so he hit me on the back. I wanted him charged and it was only George Douglas, our security executive, who dissuaded me. Naturally, the Press were told and I was accused of over-reaction. As he said, 'I merely tapped Mr Kelly on the shoulder because he was ignoring me.' He was simply a fan asking after my health. I was surprised when the Press told me that he was a financial adviser. Maybe he was trying to sell me insurance.

The 1993 AGM took place on 9 October. It was my turn to stand for re-election. The year before, when Farrell had been up, I saw it as an opportunity to confirm the unity (or otherwise) on the Board. So I had gone up to his office to discuss his re-election. I told him that I would support him, if he supported me in twelve months' time. With the shareholders' agreement, I did not need his support – but he needed mine because if I persuaded the other pact members to vote against him, he would be off. He knew that too, and agreed. I even offered to propose him but that was too public an alliance for him, so I didn't. I told Chris of the deal. 'Fat chance,' he said. And he was right, because Farrell came out against me the next year.

The rebels played this AGM as if it had been a great debating triumph for them, with us on the ropes as they shot home point after point. It was rather the opposite, as the following exchange between David and McCann demonstrates:

MR FERGUS McCANN: I am here as a representative of Mrs Angela McNaught of Surrey in England, who has asked me to represent her and to ask a few questions as Mr Barnett has done regarding the financial statement. I would like to follow up on this position regarding the costs expended by the Club, the money incurred, the £431,000 which is to be recovered from the developer in 199 – . . . 199 – . . . is it – . . . is it – . . . 6? I am not quite sure what you actually said. Anyway, when the developer decided to pay this: this money is shown as being collectable within one year. I would like to know who owes this money and who confirmed to the Club the money will be paid? Perhaps the auditors will be able to answer the question.

MR DAVID SMITH: The contract provides that the sum is recoverable immediately the initial funding for the contract is entered into, which we believe in the circumstance of Cambuslang going ahead would be within 12 months of the balance sheet date.

MR McCANN: Thank you, Mr Deputy Chairman. I made attempts to speak to the Managing Director of Superstadia, and also the Managing Director of the main contractor apparently, who is a participant in that group, and they are unable to tell me who will pay this £431,000: they know of no developer that has been identified.

MR SMITH: I think I am right in saying they declined to tell you who they believed would pay the money, not that they couldn't, but that they declined to.

MR McCANN: They were very open with me. They said – I can speak for the head estimator for Messrs. Higgs & Hill in London who told me directly that this deal has gone sour in the last few weeks, and everyone is running round in circles trying to make money, but there is nothing concrete.

MR SMITH: It is very strange that before the conversations took place with you calls were made to me to ask me to authorise any discussion with you. Those calls were made, and I made it quite clear the nature of the information that should be provided for you. I would say it is rather strange, because my understanding is that Higgs & Hill were not involved in the development.

MR McCANN: I found them very helpful and very open and very co-operative: I didn't see any problem.

MR SMITH: I instructed them to be open and co-operative: thank you.

MR McCANN: They couldn't give me any definitive answer.

MR SMITH: I have already said my understanding is that Higgs & Hill were not involved in the original development, so it would be very surprising if they were able to give you an answer.

MR McCANN: What they did tell me was that they would be very interested in developing Celtic Park, and so did the Managing Director of Superstadia.

MR SMITH: I think it is fair to say that every construction company in the country has expressed an interest in developing Celtic Park and indeed Cambuslang. You will be aware that the contract the Club entered into with Superstadia gave them the right to participate in the development at Celtic Park or Cambuslang.

MR McCANN: Mr Broughton, the Managing Director of Superstadia, told me that none of their stadiums – none of the series of stadiums they had planned or hoped to create throughout the country had been definitively funded or had any go-ahead in place, and there was a better chance of some of the smaller stadiums occurring, but the largest, the one in Cambuslang, was only a remote possibility.

MR SMITH: I am absolutely certain that Mr Broughton to whom you referred did not say that, Mr McCann. He has recorded the conversation he had with you, and I can assure you he did not say that.

MR McCANN: The conversation was very direct and open, and he did most of the talking. There was no problem.

MR SMITH: I understand it was open and straightforward, but you should not misrepresent him, because he did not say it.

MR McCANN: I can only tell you the sense that I received was that there was no definitive developer in place, they were very keen and bullish about it, but nothing definite had been concluded. That is all I would like to say, Mr Smith.

MR SMITH: So that the sense has changed from being a remote possibility, which you are suggesting he stated, it is now the centre of the conversation. Would you accept he did not say it was a remote possibility?

MR McCANN: I can't remember every word Mr Broughton said over a period of twenty minutes, but I can tell you this:

he told me that nothing definitive had developed. These people are promoters, and they want to see something happen, and they were very bullish about it, but nevertheless nothing definitive or organised was obtained.

MR SMITH: I understand exactly the nature of what you described to me. Could I remind you that you said Mr Broughton told you it was a remote possibility.'

By the time of the EGM, Lou Macari had been appointed manager and we had beaten Rangers at Ibrox.

We also easily beat off the legal challenge to the shareholders' agreement when the Court of Session refused to grant the interim interdict that the rebels sought. Dempsey realised that this was the end and let it out that he was leaving to pursue business interests in the States. In the middle of November 1993, it was announced that he was going to buy a football club over there. 'The deal is expected to be concluded in the next month,' he said. But Dempsey promised in the Press that 'if we win control I will stay'. He didn't buy the club and he didn't stay.

The EGM on 26 November 1993 was to consider the familiar McCann package: an injection of capital, he to have 51% and the shares to be issued at £60. As the shares had been changing hands at £350, no director could support such a proposal. After a predictable victory for the Board, Dempsey declared that he had 'spoken to McCann and it is the end of the road for us. There is nothing further we can do other than to walk away from it all'. A very different interpretation is given by Low, who writes: 'Dempsey and McCann had announced their withdrawal but had simply pulled back out of sight awaiting the moment they knew would come.' And, in an exclusive interview with McCann on 25 May 1994, the *Celtic View* revealed that he had not been pulling out at all: 'McCann flew back to Montreal *knowing* he would return later to put his plan into effect.' Why all the deception?

It was touch and go whether David and I would make the meeting. Teresa – my daughter, the doctor – was graduating that day from the Royal College of Obstetricians and Gynaecologists in London and, EGM or not, Zita and I were determined to be there. After the graduation, David picked us up in central London and we headed for Heathrow. We made the four-fifteen shuttle easily. But the plane sat on the ground for over an hour delayed by fog.

We made the meeting with twenty minutes to spare. Going into the meeting, bricks were thrown at Zita and afterwards four men challenged Mandy – my daughter, the lawyer. We had already had a death threat to the house, and on New Year's morning an Irish voice phoned to threaten to bomb our home.

Even at times like this, I was determined not to let these people get to us and I occasionally attempted to lighten the atmosphere by playing silly jokes. The most effective was after the November 1993 EGM. The next day, a Saturday, I phoned our solicitor, Elspeth Campbell, at her office, and, doing my world-famous Fergus McCann impression, I demanded that she arrange a meeting with Michael Kelly. She was completely taken in.

The Press campaign took a new twist with the *Evening Times* declaring 'Board may be set to dump Michael', ignoring the fact that it is shareholders in general meeting, not directors, who remove or appoint directors, and I had just been re-elected for a further three years a few weeks earlier. But it was all part of the attempt to debilitate us.

On 29 December 1993 the rebels who had 'gone away' just one month earlier were said to be planning another meeting in the Cayman Islands. No one commented on or criticised the U-turn.

Chapter Ten

They looked back, all th' eastern gate beheld,
Of Paradise, so late their happy seat . . .

Paradise Lost, 1.641

At two minutes past three on 1 January 1994, Alexis Michaili-
chenkov put the ball past Pat Bonner and Rangers went two up
in the Ne'erday game. Celtic's challenge for the League ended
then. The scenes at Celtic Park were ugly with the fans' nurtured
hostility, exacerbated by a third goal in twenty minutes, targeted
at the Directors' Box.

As with most of Celtic's triumphs and disasters the final show-
down was precipitated by a performance against Rangers. After
this humiliating defeat the pressure was increased ten-fold. But
David was able to tell Kevin that the funding package was close
to being achieved. He had already told me, but he wanted it kept
under wraps until it was finally secured. I warned him not to tell
Kevin, who I knew would not keep the secret. But he felt that the
chairman had to know. Kevin went straight out and announced
it in a television interview: 'We are so close to making this major
announcement it is not real.' Kevin gave his own deadline of 'a
week at most', and seven days later got predictably crucified. It
was this blunder that finished David with Kevin, so that he stopped
briefing him. The result was that, in March 1994, with the bank
panicking Kevin, David let him stew. And Kevin did his deal with
the rebels.

Throughout January, there was a frenzy of takeover speculation, with new bidders being announced every week. Dempsey
was not one to miss out on this, so he gave yet another interview
to BBC Radio Scotland, part of which I reproduce here:

DAVID BEGG: Brian Dempsey, we have had a number of calls
to the BBC this week from people involved in the Scottish game
suggesting that there is to be major developments in the off-field

running of Celtic Football Club. I wonder if you know what the substance of that thought might be?

BRIAN DEMPSEY: I don't know – it is certainly not coming from our side. I know there have been a lot of rumours invading Glasgow this week about many things, but I can assure you it is not coming from anything from within my own side.

BEGG: Specifically people suggested that perhaps there is about to be, or there has been indeed, a movement in the major holding of shares involving if we can call it, the Kelly-White dynasty. Do you know of this?

DEMPSEY: No, I don't . . .

BEGG: Could it be that the directors together, while they really have got to offer it to one another within the terms of the pact, have all decided that they have all had enough and now these shares might move into other areas, would you be interested, would you be part of that?

DEMPSEY: No. One, I don't think that is the case because I don't think it is the case they have had enough. Two, I have no doubt that anyone on our side of the fence would not do it that way.

BEGG: Brian, at the time of the EGM you said that if it didn't go your way or the way of, if I can call them again, the 'rebel' shareholding group, you would walk away from the situation, you had had enough – perhaps, I think, even for all time. What is your current situation?

DEMPSEY: We are away.

BEGG: Will you come back?

DEMPSEY: Possibly, we said this. But, no, here was the truth. We said on the Saturday of the press conference "No more public hostility, no more public antipathy, we had done the best we could, we are not here to damage Celtic." I said there reaches a point where you start damaging what you are trying to protect. I felt we had reached that point . . . if a phone call came from the bank we would come back and discuss the matter . . . we are not trying to buy shares, we are not trying to create a market in shares, we are not trying to sell shares, we are not trying to do anything about shares . . . the money could be put back in place . . . it didn't mean Brian Dempsey had to be a director.

BEGG: What do you think the fans should do about a boy-cott?

DEMPSEY: I have always said a boycott doesn't solve the problem, and that is a contradiction in terms.

BEGG: . . . isn't the boycott a very sharp means of bringing this thing to a head?

DEMPSEY: Unquestionably. If I really wanted to drive the nail home, I should be calling for a boycott . . . I will put my money behind Fergus McCann, I don't necessarily have to be here, I am not searching for a directorship, not searching for ego, not searching for a board position.

We now know that, at this very time, Grant and Kevin were negotiating in secret with the rebels. Yet Dempsey had no difficulty in concealing from the interviewer (and therefore the public) what was really going on. Also going on were the not-so-secret discussions between David and the Weisfeld/Haughey camp. The Press preferred to deal in rumour-mongering.

On 10 February 1994 the *Evening Times* announced that the Board was 'ready to sell'. I was said to be the stumbling block: 'The other members of the pact are ready to sell but he is reported to be "stubbornly arrogant", believing that he will lose face if he is forced to give up his family's tradition with the Club.'

The next day the back page headline in the *Record* was 'KELLY GIVES IN'. The papers now were simply filling space with the most dramatic stories that they could dream up. The same day we were told that Rod Stewart was making a bid!

Then the *Evening Times*, having decided and announced that the Board wanted to sell, took their own story forward by reporting the fans as furious that we were bailing out for cash.

But the hand of the rebel press machine was clearly seen in the storylines that began to emerge. *Scotland on Sunday* broadened its attack from the Board to the new threat to the favoured rebels – Haughey and Weisfeld. Their 'attempted takeover could bring fresh strife instead of peace. If [they] succeed in winning control they can expect to face an EGM from Fergus'. So it was confirmed what I suspected from the first time that the rebel consortium had been announced: it wasn't for the benefit of Celtic, it was to put a particular gang in power. And their pals in the Press weren't going to let *another* group, who had more money and more relevant business experience, snatch the prize from them at this late stage.

The article went on to attack the Board. Based on the totally false assumption that we all wanted to sell – an assumption the reporters never tested with me – the article said: 'The board have undermined their own position. The majority of directors in the pact have demonstrated that they are opposed to investment but in favour of making a personal profit from their shares. Henceforth it will be impossible for them to claim that they are custodians of the Club.'

But the attack on the rival camp continued in the *Evening Times*. McCann called the other proposed takeover 'crazy'. Crazy because it properly directed at shareholders a bid of £300 per share compared to his £60.

The Press reflected the distorted scenario which the rebels invented: that the pact wanted out and were selling to Haughey for personal profit. They totally ignored the fact that Haughey's plans for the Club appeared to be far more soundly based than their own brilliant strategy . . . a strategy which consisted merely of grabbing control.

What really went on was very different. The New Year defeat did mean that attendances would fall off. When it was followed by an early exit from the Cup against Motherwell and the build-up of the organised boycott, the financial implications were serious. The assumptions on which the cash flow had been predicted, though conservative, did not allow for this bad a scenario. Without the bank doing anything, the agreement that we had with it concerning the reduction of the overdraft level would begin to exert its own pressure. Despite our best efforts to produce a conclusion to the funding question, Cambuslang had been dragging on, month after month, with promises of progress but nothing tangible.

The impression has been deliberately fostered that the pressure from the bank arose out of a deteriorating trading position. The opposite was the truth; the profitability of the company in 1993/94 had continued the improvement first shown in 1992/93. As far as that earlier year was concerned, an independent report by accountants Price Waterhouse confirmed that we had significantly improved the position. They reported turnover up and costs down. One of PW's partners, Ian Dewar, commented: 'Things were getting better for Celtic. . . . For the year currently under review things got better. . . . From the figures it looks like the previous management had got things under control to a large extent. Borrowings had come down which will have surprised some people because many thought they were going up . . . They

144

increased their turnover against the trend . . . so Celtic's increase
. . . is very creditable.'

The improvement was maintained the next year. Specifically, the management accounts for January 1994 show an operating profit of £262,000 and a surplus on the transfer account of £1,086,000, giving a trading profit for the year to date (from 1 July 1993) of £1,348,000. The comparable figures for the year to date at the end of January 1993 were an operating loss of £874,000 made up of a trading loss of £192,000 and a deficit on the transfer account of £682,000.

The turnround was achieved quite simply. It involved better control of costs and ensuring that only commercial activities that would show a return were fostered. There was much more attention to detail and with reduced staff numbers much more effective use of the excellent managers who were there and committed. Thus, between 1993 and 1994, the marketing management costs were reduced from £183,000 to £78,000, while the contribution to profits of the catering division rose from £19,000 to £108,000. The shops, which turned in a loss of £13,000 at January 1993, were now in profit to the extent of £84,000. And the value of sponsorships had increased from £517,000 to £633,000.

Despite the changes in accounting procedures under which the 1994 accounts have been prepared this improvement can still be discerned in the published accounts. No detail is given of the exceptional operating expense of £528,457 headed 'compensation costs in relation to former employees', which in effect throws the accounts into loss. Apart from payments to Stoke, Brady and Cassidy (most of whose settlement had been provided for in the previous year's accounts) the old Board did not incur these costs. So blaming the old regime for the current trading position of the Club does not stand up to scrutiny. Any further investigation will dismiss the contention that refusal to accept McCann's flawed proposals in November 1993 damaged anyone, in particular shareholders who later were able to realise much more than the £60 per share that McCann was suggesting. Incidentally, accounts prepared under the more favourable conventions now adopted would have shown the old Board making a trading profit in January of £1,694,000.

However, back then it was clear that the position would get worse over the remaining months of the season. It was clear that we would need an injection of capital – but this was to be tied to Cambuslang. As the announcement of that project

145

kept getting pushed back, so did the timing of the raising of the equity.

David began developing options. The first was to allow the shareholders to sell their shares. As a director's first duty is to the company's shareholders, this was not only a sensible route to explore but one that the law required. However, it was viewed with the utmost suspicion by Grant, always one to look for ulterior motives. He was convinced by the rebels that David was determined to sell only to one particular group, Weisfeld and Haughey. In fact, David had no such preference, and indeed never sought a buyer.

Rather, Willie Haughey, following his public offer to me of £350 a share at the 1993 AGM, had privately contacted David on behalf of himself and Weisfeld before Christmas. Discussions went on from that time as David tried to manoeuvre a rather vague approach to the position where it was 'there', to use David's word. Haughey also approached Grant, with Haughey reporting these conversations to David. Grant's response was encouraging – until he asked if he could stay on as a director after selling his shares. Haughey came back with the condition that acceptance of the offer must involve all of the pact members resigning. After that, Grant never phoned Haughey again.

David's concern was particularly for the majority shareholders – and especially Chris, Grant, Kevin and Adele Daly (Chris's aunt) – who stood to lose considerable amounts of money if they were prevented from realising the value of their shares. A lot of the discussions with Haughey were aimed at expanding the offer, which was originally made only to the directors personally, to our families and to those who had been faithful to Celtic for over three years. None of the three of us was going to see them left locked in if we were forced to walk away.

All through this period I kept urging David to conclude the financial deal on Cambuslang, because the last thing that I wanted to do was to sell to anybody. I had no preference for whom I didn't want to sell to. I knew from meetings with McCann that he was no answer to Celtic's problems. Equally, I couldn't believe that selling to Weisfeld was the correct way to end the struggle for Celtic's soul, although he had a much firmer grip on reality. Either way was a sell-out of the principles we were seeking to defend.

David himself saw Cambuslang as the other option and the

solution, but he kept saying to me: 'It isn't there. It just isn't there.' 'Get it there,' I urged him. The choice was becoming starker, and all through January the time-scale for making a decision got shorter and shorter.

On the evening of 3 February 1994, Chris phoned me and asked me to come to his house. He told me he had considered all the options and was now 'of a mind to sell'. He had had enough. He felt that the time gap between the present situation and the putting into place of the finance for Cambuslang was too long. It could not be bridged with the present mood of the support, the abysmal performance of the team and the position at the bank. He went on to say that he had spoken to Kevin that afternoon and that he, too, agreed that acceptance of Haughey's offer was inevitable.

I was appalled, but could hardly fault Chris's logic. He stood to realise around £900,000 from the sale of his shares, and the prospects for achieving Cambuslang were certainly not immediate. He also put his finger on why he was giving up. He was prepared to accept what I was not – that the campaign which had been mounted against us had produced such hostility that no matter what we did it would not be believed or accepted. All everybody wanted was for us to go. I expressed the view that this meant abandoning everything that we had fought for, at great personal cost and sacrifice. But I didn't push him too hard. He had a lot of money at stake, I had much less.

I readily agreed to go along with what David would recommend and what Chris would decide. Although David and I had long discussions about the way forward, they never developed into arguments. Until the very end there was never any question that the three of us would do other than act together. This showed tremendous loyalty on Chris's part and that of his aunt, both of whom, being such large shareholders, could have done separate deals – particularly with Mrs Daly's shares which were not in Celtic Nominees Ltd, the voting trust.

Coming home in the car, I phoned David and told him how depressed Chris's decision had left me. I urged, cajoled, exhorted him to find another way. He felt exactly as I did, but was doubtful if he could pull Cambuslang together in time. He committed himself to keep trying. But he was becoming increasingly pessimistic about the prospects of firming up the deal in time. So he called a meeting in Grant's house on 5 February, the morning of the Raith Rovers away game.

At that meeting David was at his lucid best, clearly outlining exactly what the financial position of the Club would be two months down the road in the context of the current performance on the field and its effect on attendances. He emphasised how little time we had to find a solution. Both Grant and Kevin were deeply shocked and agreed after a fairly long consideration that, in the circumstances that David had outlined, acceptance of the Haughey/Weisfeld offer was the sensible step. There is no doubt that Kevin went fully along with this proposition. Grant agreed to it, too, but for the first time was making his new-found antipathy to Haughey clear.

Then David outlined the alternative – Cambuslang. He proposed and got agreement for the plan that was later outlined at the press conference on 25 February 1994. Indeed, there was great excitement for and enthusiasm about the prospect because David, in his eloquent way, had drawn the parallel with the proposed Celtic structure and Manchester United, with its separation of public and Club Boards. So it was agreed: David would make one final attempt to fund Cambuslang and on its back Celtic would go public with none of the existing directors expecting to be represented on the Board of the new public company. In the immediate term there would be an issue of shares to raise £3m of capital – but that again depended on Cambuslang.

On the way through to Kirkcaldy, Kevin announced to the car that we should have a royal opening of Cambuslang, a curious suggestion. Then he delivered the punchline: the stadium was to be opened by the Duchess of Kent! I thought it worth re-telling this to Grant at the game. 'Magic,' he said, 'and David can look after the Duke!' Now, if you do not understand either of these two allusions, you can congratulate yourself – because you have not been invaded by the virus of prejudice that still infects the West of Scotland.

Another example manifested itself at half-time. Scotland's rugby team were playing for the Calcutta Cup that day and I had made the Raith Rovers' secretary put on the television so that we could watch the final few minutes. Scotland were just ahead as we joined the coverage, but lost just on the final whistle. As I got to the top of the stairs on the way back to my seat, the PA system broadcast the news of Scotland's last-minute, one-point defeat. The Celtic supporters in the stand burst out cheering and taunting the Raith Rovers fans behind the goal. It was almost as depressing as watching the play to try and work out their thought-processes. 'And these are the guys that are passing judgment on me,' crossed my mind.

An integral part of David's proposal was to raise £3 million in equity very quickly, to satisfy the Club's short-term requirements. He needed this underwritten and was confident that this would be achieved. The availability of the capital funds for the stadium's construction would be crucial in this: Nally would not move until he had an indication from the Swiss bank that he was dealing with that they would provide support.

David left me to draft a press release that would announce Cambuslang, a public confirmation that he was developing both options vigorously and fully. But he was not at all confident that he could swing things. Indeed, he kept emphasising that the Weisfeld offer was the best alternative solution. I kept urging him to make one more effort, quoting to him from Willie Maley's book about the history of Celtic to try to inspire him. He brought his copy to the phone and we swapped quotations. I then resorted to *Field of Dreams*, exhorting him to 'go the distance'. Melodramatic it seems now. It didn't then. Low, in his book, sneers at our using this baseball film's title for Cambuslang. But then he would. That film captured the essence and romance and emotional appeal of America's national sport. It raised it above business and commerce to nobler ideals. That was how we viewed our mission with Celtic. The rebels could never share these aspirations.

One night that week Kevin phoned me with a solution. Businessmen (John Keane and Jim Torbett were mentioned) had been in touch. They wanted to support him. 'There should always be a Kelly at Celtic Football Club,' they had told him. They would put up the money. We wouldn't have to accept Weisfeld's offer. I would have to go, but I would be off the Board anyway so that didn't matter. When I came off the phone I didn't know which to laugh at first: the notion that he could believe that there was anyone who genuinely would put up money to support him, or the naïvely straightforward way he thought I would be delighted to support a solution that included me out, but left him sitting there!

149

On Friday 18 February 1994, at three forty-five in the afternoon, David phoned me in the car to tell me to be at a meeting at Dickson Minto's in Edinburgh at six o'clock. I was not at all keen because I could see it being one of those long, rambling Celtic meetings that would go on for hours without a conclusion. David told me that it was essential to meet, to ensure that the Haughey/Weisfeld offer was unconditional and backed by money in a Dickson Minto client account. I had no intention of selling, so the meeting seemed a bit of a charade to me – especially as I had been drafting and re-drafting the Cambuslang press release and had been in touch with the Club's solicitors, collaborating in the preparation of the circular necessary to call the EGM to approve the necessary shares issue.

But David insisted that it was part of the policy of keeping all options open that the offer should actually be seen to be there. Whether we accepted it or not was another matter. David told me to get Kevin and Grant there as well. I phoned Kevin at home from the car. He said he could not come because he was going to Hawick for the weekend. I broke off the conversation because the mobile line was bad, went straight into the house and re-dialled. I was given the message that he had left. He was out of contact for the whole weekend!

I then phoned Grant several times. He clearly did not want to go, feeling that the purpose of the meeting was to browbeat him and Kevin into accepting the offer. He told me that David had explained the seriousness of the bank position to him, but that he (Grant) believed that it had been exaggerated. It was all part of David's tactic to put pressure on him. He then said that, if he went, it would only be to listen and not to make a decision. I told him that would be fine, as I was not going to make a decison myself. Then he said that he would not go and advised me not to, either: 'If you go it will be the worst decision of your life.'

I phoned David, told him that neither of them would go and that, in the circumstances, there was little point in my trailing through. He then revealed that Haughey would be present at Dickson Minto's, though not necessarily at the meeting. That confirmed my decision. There was one thing I could not have faced that Friday night, or indeed any Friday night, and that was a dose of Willie Haughey. Chris had already left and, as Celtic did not supply a car phone, could not be stopped. I phoned Grant back to tell him that I had decided not to go, and he congratulated me. That phone call was probably what made them treat me differently from David and Chris at their meeting on 3 March.

It is now clear that, by this time, Grant and Kevin must have been talking to, indeed receiving instructions from, the rebels. Grant began expressing stronger and stronger hostility towards Haughey. 'What will it do for the team?' he asked me. I got the impression that what he could not stomach about Haughey was that he was a of a similar type and background to himself. The difference was that Haughey had made a lot of money. Grant couldn't stand the thought of his taking over. The rebels had obviously managed to play on his insecurity to convince him that a deal was being done behind his back. It wasn't.

I had told Zita that David was now recommending that we had to get out. She and Maureen were in tears when I came back into the room. No one wanted to sell.

What I did not find out that night was that a letter from the bank had been delivered to Chris at Celtic Park last thing on Friday afternoon. Chris did not open the letter until he came into the office on the Saturday morning. He then spent the weekend trying to contact Kevin – without success as calls to the Hawick number that he left were not returned. My sister Maureen also tried to contact Kevin, with the same lack of success. She had heard on the television that Kevin had been in contact with Dempsey in America and wanted to establish the truth of it. Later, Kevin assured me that he had not been in touch when, of course, he had.

On Monday 21 February 1994 Chris asked to meet Kevin, Grant and me. Chris read out the bank letter. It included a reference to the fact that the purchase of Willie Falconer temporarily took the overdraft over the limit. Basically, what the bank was saying very clearly was that the company had an overdraft limit and must ensure that it was adhered to. But it was saying no more than that.

In view of the serious general tone of the letter, I was surprised that the point Grant leapt on was the Willie Falconer deal. But, having established that it was David who authorised it, his suspicion became clear. He believed that David was deliberately worsening the cash position to force the Haughey/Weisfeld's offer on to us.

This offer was discussed in the light of the meeting that Chris

151

had had on the Friday. Chris wanted to sell and informed us that David supported him in this. I made it clear that I did not want to sell. Grant made great play about wanting to see the documentation before he could discuss it any further. So it was faxed from Dickson Minto's and a copy given to each of us. Kevin and Grant left the Park, presumably to consult the rebels. I took my copy home where it lay in its envelope unopened. I was not going to sell unless forced to, and then the precise conditions would not really matter.

The next morning, Tuesday 22 February 1994, the full voting trust convened in Chris's Bath Street office at ten o'clock. Grant brought his own lawyer who sat in an outer office the whole of the morning. I wondered who was going to pay for him. Grant had got Celtic to pay his legal fees in relation to the first EGM, so I couldn't see him stumping up money at this late stage. The start of the meeting was delayed because Kevin was late. It had snowed unexpectedly that morning and he had gone to Celtic Park by mistake! That was what he *said*.

The meeting was kicked off by Grant announcing that the offer was not a bona fide one. I still don't know what he meant by that, but was not interested in pursuing it because I was not there to talk about its acceptance. Options were discussed. It was quite clear that no one really wanted to sell. Grant and Kevin were very hostile to Haughey/Weisfeld. David, Chris and I argued for selling because, with the threat from the bank increasing, it seemed that there was no alternative. I was trying to think of the shareholders who had kept faith with us. Using my cousin Yvonne as an example, I asked Grant how he could explain to her turning down an offer of £300 a share.

We then discussed whether Cambuslang had any chance at all of being delivered in the short time that we had. We all reaffirmed our feeling of 5 February that, if it could be made to happen, it was best way forward. David agreed to try again, particularly with the underwriting of the rights issue.

We then adjourned for lunch. David and Chris went off somewhere and I went back to my office. Grant phoned me there – from home, he said, where he had gone to talk things over with his wife. By chance, Maureen was in my office and was a witness to the conversation. Grant told me that if he could be shown that the Haughey deal offered something for Club then he would not block it. He mentioned my argument

152

about Yvonne and said that he 'did not want to do the woman out of her money'. I believed that he was utterly honest in the sentiments that he was expressing. I was equally straight with him. I told him that the consensus that we had reached in the morning was that we go with Cambuslang. I did not want to accept any offer, and did not see that selling to Haughey and Weisfeld could be said to be meeting our obligations to Celtic.

We reconvened after lunch for Chris to tell us that he had secured £1 million of underwriting and for David to announce what I already knew, that he had secured £1.5 million. David then read out the draft circular for the proposed EGM. He had asked me to start work on this weeks earlier and had had it approved by the solicitors, who were also working on the circular for the EGM – all part of his policy of developing fully every possible option. It was decided, on the strength of the £2.5 million of underwriting, that the rights issue would be announced on the Friday – provided that the final go-ahead for Cambuslang had been given by then.

As we were leaving, Grant's main worry was what story he was going to spin his pals in the rebel camp until Friday. We left him to his worry.

Grant and Kevin were doorstepped by Allan Caldwell and Scottish Television on leaving the meeting. Kevin was seen on television saying: 'There is no split.'

I left with David and walked him round to the bank. I wanted to go in with him, but he suggested that it was better that I didn't. I now wish that I had, because it would have given me personally a flavour of Rowland Mitchell's demeanour. David came round to my office later to tell me that the bank had now been told of the proposal and that he would be working on it. He invited Mitchell to the Board meeting that we planned for the Friday afternoon.

On Wednesday 23 February 1994, the bank was again on the phone to Chris wanting to know what the reaction of the directors to their letter was and wanting to know what we proposed to do. When I raised this with David, he told me that he had spoken to the bank again and that they were not happy. He was confident, however, that he could handle it. Late the same day the bank delivered to Chris individual letters for distribution to the directors, calling for personal guarantees.

Later, the bank also phoned Kevin, who then phoned Chris. Chris told him precisely what the position was. Then Grant phoned Chris and asked: 'What's this about the bank wanting personal guarantees by Monday?'

These noises from the bank were worrying me, but David was looking after that side of things and I was confident of both his ability and of the relationship that he had with the bank.

On Thursday 24 February, work continued on putting Cambuslang and the underwriting for the share issue together. I stayed on late at the office, re-drafting the news release with Mike Stanger, whom I told of the plan for the first time. Mike, who had known of the connection with Gefinor since November, expressed surprise and concern that they were to be identified in the news release, but I confirmed that this was to be done.

Grant phoned me several times, concerned that the package would not be pulled together. The Press later told me he was expecting to go in next day to be told that, despite all efforts, Cambuslang had failed and that we must accept Haughey's offer. He obviously suspected that Cambuslang was now merely a diversionary tactic, to demonstrate that David and Chris had tried their best before selling to Haughey.

But on the same day, Nally's firm, Stadivarious (part of the Superstadia consortium) at last got in writing the assurances on funding that had been so long in coming. Gefinor had confirmed their agreement to provide a conditional letter of guarantee for £20 million to the contractor appointed to build the new multi-purpose stadium at Cambuslang. Nally also warned that the Gefinor culture was against high public exposure and, while they could be identified, we must be cautious about how we used their name. On the same day Nally indicated that he was now eager to participate in the underwriting, to the extent of £1.5 million, of the new equity.

On Friday 25 February 1994, I was at Celtic Park early to show Grant and Kevin the press release while we waited for David and Nally to arrive off the same plane from London. They travelled in the same car to Celtic Park. Questioned by Grant and Kevin, Nally was confident and confirmed that all of the financial details were in place.

The announcement at the press conference astonished everyone. David was determined that it should be chaired properly and not be the usual blundering, stumbling affair that we had to endure at AGMs and EGMs. So he took the chair and told me to provide only one other at the top table, for Nally. But Kevin wandered down to the front behind them and, pulling over a chair, sat very uncomfortably at the corner of the table.

David's announcement delivered to the Press and fans everything that they claimed needed to be changed at Celtic Park. I can do no better than quote the Press Release:

CELTIC CONFIRMS 21st CENTURY VISION

Far-Reaching Proposals to Transcend Factions

David Smith, Deputy Chairman of Celtic Football Club, today announced a comprehensive and visionary package of radical measures designed to take the club into a glittering new future in the 21st century.

• The club will move to a new state-of-the-art stadium complex at Cambuslang. Cornerstone funding of £20 million has now been committed, enabling the project to move forward to secure detailed planning permission and then to construction.

• The capital structure of the club will be totally recast. The authorised share capital will be increased by 25,000 shares. The majority of the available shares will be issued at a price significantly in excess of the £60 per share proposed at last November's EGM. This will raise up to £6 million. Notice of an EGM for this purpose will be given next week. The funds will be used to reduce borrowing and to strengthen the team.

• The club will 'go public' towards the end of this year, and a Stock Exchange listing sought, to enable its shares to be freely traded. This will allow a range of investors, from individuals to institutions, to participate in ownership of the club.

• A new Board of Directors will be appointed for 'Celtic PLC', drawn from the ranks of those used to conducting the affairs of a public company and responsible to the new shareholders. The majority of the existing directors do not anticipate serving on that Board, but some may become members of a Club Board whose primary role will be to ensure that the traditions, spirit and values of the Club are safeguarded.

David Smith says: 'These proposals transcend past and present factions and family interests, and will provide supporters and financial backers with a completely new concept of how a football club should be run in the modern world.'

The proposals are underpinned by the central announcement that £20 million of cornerstone funding from the private sector has been secured for the Cambuslang Stadium project. Patrick Nally, the funding adviser to the project, today revealed that the underwriting is being provided by Gefinor, an international merchant bank.

The Cambuslang project now comprises a stadium of more than 40,000 seated capacity, and an associated indoor arena with a spectator capacity of some 10,000. The latter will be suitable for a range of activities including concerts, ice hockey, basketball and equestrian events. These two elements of the development will be owned by Celtic PLC. The Club has already been invited to run major ice hockey and basketball teams.

David Smith says: 'With this unprecedented and far-reaching package of measures, Celtic will be put into a position to compete in a football world which we expect to be very different from the present.

'A crucial element of the proposed public offering will be the clear separation of the public company and its management of the Club. A similar model already exists in the organisation of Manchester United.

'This route will reconcile the different aspirations of everyone with a genuine concern for, and a legitimate interest in, the future of Celtic – supporters, shareholders, willing investors and others. None of the proposals put forward by others meet those different interests in such a constructive and exciting manner.'

Patrick Nally adds: 'The Cambuslang stadium is the most challenging funding project I have ever been involved in. Throughout the nine months since achieving outline planning permission, we have reviewed and amended our ideas in order to make sure that we have produced the best possible scheme for one of the world's great clubs.'

With reference to recent, unfounded speculation, David Smith said that he was not aware of any director who has sought a buyer for his current shareholding. 'I know that over the last two years, numerous unsolicited approaches have been made to individual directors to sell their shares, and all have been rejected.

'All of the major shareholders would rather see all available funds invested in the new Celtic.'

David had also ensured that Weisfeld was informed of our decision before the press anouncement. He faxed him in Australia to say that Cambuslang would go ahead as 'the core funding is in place and the scheme is viable'. He went on to confirm that there was an 'immediate commitment to seeking public flotation when Cambuslang construction commences and certainly within 1994'. His fax concluded: 'At its simplest it provides a realistic, credible and inspiring way ahead for everyone who wants to put something into the Club, whether financial or otherwise and no comfort of any kind for someone who wants to take something out.'

During the questioning after David's announcement, Kevin was asked if it was true that he would be happy to resign from the main Board to allow more appropriate directors to serve. He said that he would. But his eyes told a different story. Grant backed up the proposal to the Press afterwards, being very supportive in interviews.

Our announcement, apart from answering all the questions that we had been asked and being precisely the right thing for Celtic, created a huge problem for the rebels. We were going to raise between £4 and £6 million and we had at least half of it underwritten. The door that had been slammed in their faces by the shareholders' agreement was now bolted tight. Those of them who were shareholders (McCann wasn't) had to decide whether or not to stay with the action and subscribe to the issue to avoid being diluted. Even if they did they were still going to be in a minority position in the short run. When the whole plan had been brought to fruition later in 1994, all of the existing shareholders would be marginalised in the public company. Control by us or them would have been removed from the agenda. The fans would have a voice *and* a vote.

The media were totally enraged by the announcement. It contradicted everything that they had been claiming, although it gave them all that they claimed they wanted for the Club –

except us out and McCann and Dempsey in. So, naturally, the Press reacted violently against it.

Alan Davidson and Ken Symon were clearly following the tradition at the *Evening Times* and rubbished the whole announcement – their comments were set on the page almost before the news conference began.

The Press decided that we had to go. Announcing the Cambuslang funding package was: 'A last act of treachery, betrayal and treason [sic], the last throw of the dice by a desperate group of men . . . determined to cling to power, can't possibly have any more dirty tricks hidden up their grubby sleeves.' Or so went the verdict of Graham Clark of the *Sun*, whose editorial summed up what the issue now was: ' . . . they've missed the point. They could have come up with a cast-iron plan to resurrect Celtic . . . But the fans still wouldn't have wanted to be part of it.' The Press refused to evaluate the proposals on their merits. They wheeled on Charlie Nicholas, who manages his own financial affairs so well, to tell the world it was all claptrap: 'Basically, it is all business jargon that means nothing to the ordinary man in the street . . .' Goodness knows what he and other ordinary men have made of McCann's pronouncements since then.

The next day, on Radio Clyde, I had the most ridiculous interchange with Hugh Keevins. He kept asking me if Celtic owned the ground at Cambuslang. I kept trying to give him the answer, which was that we had an option to buy it, an option we didn't have to exercise until we knew that the development was actually going ahead. But he wanted 'yes' or 'no' for an answer, and continued to demand one or the other response. I said, 'You can't always answer every question truthfully with "yes" or "no".' He insisted you could. There are two answers, he said: 'Which one is it? "Yes" or "no"?'

Faced with this absurdity I said: 'Have you stopped beating your wife, Hugh? Yes or no?' 'No,' came the reply, 'certainly not!' I asked if that was true. 'Of course it's not!' he went on, equally sure. 'You mean, you tell lies?' I suggested. 'Yes,' he said, 'all the time.' Incredible.

There was, in between the knee-jerk whines from people who hadn't bothered to keep in touch with both sides, some grudging admiration for the proposals, and an acknowledgement – even from Kevin McCarra in *Scotland on Sunday* – that they might work. But it was left to Roddy Forsyth in the *Telegraph* papers to stand back and give full and fair credit to David's master plan, on which he had done so much work, especially over the previous six months.

But the reaction from the rebels demonstrated that they were only in the fight to get control. Our announcement had produced the long-term solution. It had also delivered answers to all of the criticisms made of the Club. In particular, the Board would go and the Club would become a public company – two of things that we had been profoundly and persistently criticised for resisting. Yet could we find anyone to welcome the proposals? Of course not. The rebels didn't want this solution which was right for Celtic. They wanted to be in charge. Every time I went on radio and television in the week after the press conference I asked if all of the things that we had proposed were good and desirable. Why then were they being attacked? There was no answer. But the attacks continued.

The only criticism that might have had any validity was that the changes needed a two-thirds majority to get through an EGM, and we only had 60%. But, with Counsel's help we had found a simple solution to that. While a two-thirds majority of shareholders was needed, only a simple majority of shares was required. And we could get both.

Under our proposal, the fans would have been able to buy shares which would have given them a voice and a vote. Under the McCann plan, put forward at the EGM on 28 April 1994, not only will the share-owning supporters be barred from voting, they won't even be entitled to attend shareholders' meetings!

The Board meeting after the news conference was duly held in the afternoon. Farrell was understandably beside himself that he hadn't been told of the conference. McGinn was philosophical. By a majority of six-to-one, Cambuslang and the share issue was agreed. We then turned to discussing the bank position. I knew that Rowland Mitchell was due to arrive and was desperate to get the discussion concluded with some agreement before he got there. But Celtic meetings have a habit of dragging on endlessly in meaningless ramblings, and Mitchell walked in before it was concluded. I wanted to keep him out until we had finished, but I think David wanted him to see for himself what we were dealing with. Mitchell, of course, asumed that everyone had seen his letter. He found it 'bizarre' that they had not been given out. He then asked for personal guarantees or the right to assign the debt and control of our shares. Grant and I resisted this very strongly. I pointed out that Celtic was as much a Scottish institution as the Bank of Scotland. The bank had supported us for 106 years. 'Make it 106 years and six weeks,' I asked, referring to the injection of equity that would come after the EGM. He agreed to wait to see the figures which were being crunched over the weekend.

I showed him out and asked for support to put our plans through. He replied that he had to sleep in his bed too, as he got into a chauffeur-driven car. I felt Mitchell had played the meeting all wrong. He should have been much calmer and more detached, instead of committing himself to a course of action which would be difficult to reverse. I got the impression, too, that Mitchell knew very little about the football business, and so what he read in the papers unduly influenced him. What he read wasn't good.

On Tuesday 1 March 1994, Mitchell was presented with the figures. He was not at all happy, but David assured me that he could be handled. Mitchell then asked Chris if he could meet the Board the following day.

We met at three o'clock, without David, at the bank's Glasgow head office. I was late, and entered a very gloomy atmosphere. Mitchell repeated that his position was unchanged from that of Friday. He had seen the figures, which showed that the overdraft would rise by a further £800,000 by the end of March. He spoke mainly to me and to Chris who were the only ones who contributed to the discussion. The others simply sat in silence. The two of us answered all the questions that he had on the projections. We pointed out that the end of March was the peak overdraft and that it would fall thereafter. But he argued that rights issues were not guaranteed and that he was not prepared to take the additional risk involved in supporting us until it had been successfully concluded. He then proposed that our shares be handed over to a firm such as Noble Grossart who would sell them at the best price on his instructions if things went wrong. This, of course, simply confirmed Grant's unfounded suspicion that Mitchell was working hand-in-glove with David to get the shares to Weisfeld. He said that he had cleared his action with the Treasurer and Gavin Masterton. I told him that I would think further about what he had said, and ended the meeting.

I had to get back to my office to deal with the Press, because our news conference had increased the criticism rather than reduced it. The Press had built up the scenario that we were leaving with large pay-offs. They weren't quite sure who was to take over. But we were going, that was for certain. They had all turned up the previous Friday to hear our resignations. They weren't about readily to forgive us for proving them wrong. When I got back, just minutes after the meeting ended, there was a message from the *Herald*, asking us to confirm the meeting at the bank.

But there was another problem: the *Evening Times* had put the cat among the pigeons with its simple front-page headline: 'What £20m?' It was a story which had to be killed, promptly, or we would never recover. Try as I did to get Patrick Nally, or anyone from Gefinor in Europe or New York to react, I couldn't. From then on, we in Glasgow were as much in the dark as anyone, possibly more so. I still don't know the full answer as to why Gefinor denied its commitment to Stadivarious. David had been satisfied because he had seen the correspondence between Gefinor and Nally. Two days later, this was shown by David's PR man to Roddy Forsyth and Geoff Webster of the BBC, to confirm its existence and authenticity. It wasn't shown more widely because of Nally's concern about Gefinor's reaction.

Gefinor had made it clear to Nally that they wanted the minimum of publicity, and that they were not geared up to deal with Press enquiries. It was therefore not surprising that they were unprepared for the assault from the Scottish Press. What did the Press care about the niceties of the different contractual arrangements? They were also unaware of the reluctance of any financier to say unequivocally – particularly in the media – that the funding is in place for any project.

Financial institutions shun publicity, but at this time, sensitivities were heightened by the case of Samuel Montagu, who were held, after a prolonged court action, to be responsible for confirming that funds were available to their client on the basis of a conversation in a private meeting.

The *Financial Times* described the circumstances as follows: 'In August 1987, Mr Ian McIntosh, then Montagu's head of corporate finance, attended a meeting of about 30 people . . . British and Commonwealth Holdings wanted a reassurance from

161

Montagu that its client had the money to complete a purchase. Mr McIntosh was asked and replied, simply: "Yes." ... Mr McIntosh was asked to give his assurance after [being told] that there was no time to prepare full documentation ... But after the acquisition, [the bank's client] failed to provide the cash ... helping drive B & C into administration.'

McIntosh's simple affirmative answer, which was merely meant as reassurance, cost the bank £172 million in damages. The *FT* went on: 'One corporate financier said it would make him far more cautious about signing "highly confident" letters in which merchant banks gave assurances that their clients were able to lay hands on funds ... "If you tell the man in the street funds are available, he understands that there is a pile of cash next door. But when a corporate financier says it, it does not mean quite the same. Most people in the City know that." ... Other bankers argued that it would be common to sign a letter with a number of disclaimers and conditions ... "such a lot of conditions that you are protected, quite frankly".'

The letter which Stadivarious had received from Gefinor was much stronger. It was conditional, but its purpose was mainly to satisfy the intended contractor that the money was there, because there was no contractual relationship between Celtic and Gefinor, nor indeed between Celtic and the contractor – nor was there intended to be. They were satisfied – not surprisingly, since they had contributed, along with David and Nally, to its drafting. Celtic, for its part, had received confirmation from Stadivarious that they had the necessary undertakings from Gefinor. To the man in the street, and the *Evening Times*, it was still not a pile of cash next door. But to the informed and financially-sophisticated participants it was the indication which was needed, for which they had been waiting for some time, and on which they knew they could rely.

The Press merely wanted to know if it was true that Gefinor were giving Celtic £20 million for a new stadium. The Gefinor responses, not surprisingly, were very reluctant. It took some cajoling to persuade them to confirm that they were involved in the project at all and that detailed documentation with Stadivarious was being put in place. They did that. But their cautious confirmation was not enough to convince a sceptical Press. More importantly, the nuances of the position were lost on Kevin and Grant, who believed what they read in the papers and fell straight into the arms of the rebels.

On the Thursday morning, Haughey phoned to ask me to meet him and Weisfeld. I arranged the meeting for four o'clock. An hour earlier, I started an interview with BBC Northern Ireland Television. During the interview a notice came from Pannell's fax machine (timed at 1641 hrs!) calling a Board meeting for 3.30pm at Pannell Kerr Forster.

It was immediately clear that we had lost control of the Board. After discussing it with David, I decided that it was better not to try to get to the Board meeting. I was already going to be late for it, and I didn't want to add a spurious authenticity to it by my presence. So Chris and I saw Weisfeld, Haughey and McDonald, as arranged, in Francis McCrossin's office. This was the first time that I had had any meetings at all with this group. Weisfeld stuck me as genuinely concerned. He displayed a firm grasp of Celtic's difficulties and a business-like approach to their solution. He emphasised that he did not want to cause Celtic further embarrassment and that he would only act with the agremeent of the Board. He did not tell us that he had offered a £3 million guarantee to the bank that morning. He repeated that, if he were to intervene to help, it would require all of the existing Board to resign. We accepted and agreed with that. He offered no special deals.

From that office, I phoned Kevin at Pannells. He told me first of all that he had tried in vain to contact David. What he did not say was that, while he left messages at Cannon Street that he was looking urgently for David, he did not leave a number where he could be contacted. That was because he was locked in with his new allies at Pannells all day (they didn't let him out of their sight) and did not want to give the game away by leaving that number. When I asked him the next week why he had not asked me to the meeting with the bank he said: 'Because I knew you would be against what we were going to do.' Surely the best reason for ensuring that I was there? But on the phone that afternoon, he went on to tell me that 'friends' had put up the £1 million guarantee that the bank were asking for. I asked him who these people were. He named John Keane, Jim Torbett, himself and Grant.

I agreed to go down to Pannells at five o'clock. I arrived at five-fifteen, expecting to meet the rest of the directors but only Kevin and Grant met me. They showed me the minutes of that afternoon's Board meeting and the letter from the bank.

Minute of Meeting of the
Directors of Celtic Football
& Athletic Company Ltd held
at 78 Carlton Place, Glasgow
on 3 March 1994 at 3.30pm.

Present: Kevin Kelly
   Jack McGinn
   James Farrell
   Tom Grant

1. The Chairman reported on the meeting held this afternoon with the Bank of Scotland concerning

(a) the current financial position of the Company.
(b) the actions of David Smith and Christopher White over   the last month.
and (c) the imminent receivership of the Company.

2. In view of the information from the Bank, it was agreed that David Smith and Christopher White be immediately stripped of all executive duties and that the resignation of David Smith and Christopher White be requested.

3. It was agreed that the Bank of Scotland be instructed that all communications from the Bank, verbal or written, to the Company be addressed only to the Chairman.

4. The Chairman reported that the Bank had advised the Company of their requirements to postpone the appointment of a Receiver as follows:

"that a Guarantee for £1m suitably secured and in a
form acceptable to the Bank be delivered to the Bank
by 12 noon 4 March 1994"

It was resolved that the requirement would be met.

Unlike normal Board minutes which are signed only by the chairman, all four conspirators had put their names to this.
The letter from the bank was as follows:

3rd March 1994

Dear Mr Kelly,

I am most grateful to you, Mr Grant, Mr McGinn, Mr Farrell and Mr Kean [sic] for the time you spared in coming to see me today. I am delighted that we seem to have identified an acceptable way forward and that, therefore, the immediate and dire peril facing the Club can be averted. I have to say that some of the disclosures made by Mr Kean [sic] on behalf of those Board members present about the operation of Celtic's affairs at Board level in the recent past were staggering.

I feel it is appropriate that I should put down on paper my understanding of the agreement we reached and of the key points of our conversation.

1) By a majority decision the Board has resolved that Mr David Smith be asked to resign forthwith.

2) To avoid any confusion in future any contracts between the Bank and the Celtic Board will be through its Chairman Mr Kevin Kelly.

3) The Bank has agreed to continue to honour cheques drawn on the Celtic Account on the following conditions:-

   a) By 12 noon tomorrow a cash collateralised or otherwise acceptably supported Guarantee for the sum of £1M is put in place to support the Club's overdraft.

   b) This Guarantee will be superseded by a £5M cash collateralised Guarantee which will be made available once Mr Fergus McCann has reached the UK and has had a chance to apprise himself of the situation, latest the middle of next week.

   c) The second Guarantee will support an overdraft facility of £7.5M, the terms of which will be negotiated with a representative of the Celtic Board.

   d) The first of these Guarantees will be unconditional save for a requirement that the Bank must have no further negotiations with any other faction interested in becoming involved in Celtic Football Club.

4) Appropriate Board Resolutions addressing the intention of

proceeding down the route outlined and identifying the specific point of contact between our two organisations will be made available immediately.

I hope that this very brief summary is a true reflection of where we stand at the moment.

I look forward to hearing from you and hopefully to a continuing relationship between our two organisations.

Yours sincerely

J. Rowland Mitchell

The bank could defend its action, but only in strictly banking terms. They wanted increased security or the loan reduced. That Thursday they were sitting with three possible sources of money: our rights issue, Weisfeld's offer and McCann's approach. But whichever one of these was to be accepted had to come through the Board. And here was a majority of the Board telling Mitchell the route that they preferred. A nervous banker need look no further.

But that is a simplistic analysis. For a start, a number of the actions proposed by the directors required shareholder action. The bank could, I suppose, argue that that was a matter for the directors not the bank. Then there were the personal relationships. The bank knew David. Indeed, the Celtic banking was run exclusively through David. I would have expected the bank to have given him some indication at some time during that Thursday of the way that things were going. Or to have asked the directors who went to the bank to inform David of that meeting. But the bank sat passively, knowing that the rest of the directors were circumventing David – and Chris, the biggest shareholder.

Of course, if Grant and Kevin had not changed sides, it would never have got to this stage. They will argue that if they had not, the company would have been put into receivership that afternoon. In my view, that would not have happened. There was an option that would have eventually satisfied the bank's requirement. That was the rights issue. Though it was a less certain solution from the bank's point of view than someone simply taking over the debt, it was one which they would have accepted if the directors had stood firmly behind it. The rebels' strategy for the past year or more had been to provide an option for the bank. It did not become credible until the four directors supported it. If Kevin alone had stood firm, it would have remained purely potential. The bank, knowing that,

166

would have only had the choice between continuing to support the Club until the rights issue was in place, or in pulling the plug. It is a question of judgment, but my opinion is that there was no chance whatsoever in those circumstances of the bank calling in the receiver.

The four directors' shame is that they did not give David the opportunity of revealing the provision that he had made for this very contingency – an immediate injection of capital – before they sold Celtic out.

The first thing I noticed from the bank's letter was that the guarantors were different from the names Kevin had told me over the phone just one hour before. The second thing that I noticed was that I had not been attacked, just Chris and David. Grant told me that the in-fighting must end. This was my chance to get behind this, he said, pointing to the minute. 'Behind what?' I asked, because I really didn't know what he was talking about or what I was being offered. I asked him because I knew Kevin wouldn't know either. 'Fergus's November proposal,' he said. 'Tom,' I said, 'I can't just abandon Chris and David now.' He shrugged. That was something he couldn't understand. There was some discussion about their buying my shares. I told them that I could not sell and leave the others – namely, Chris, David, our supporters among the smaller shareholders and the other members of Kevin's and my families – locked in. We agreed to a Board meeting the next morning at ten o'clock.

I phoned Chris's wife, Linda, who was eight months' pregnant. She was in tears because the letter suspending Chris had arrived at their home and, in Chris's absence, she had opened it.

I then went home and planned by phone the options with David. They had not yet co-opted anyone to the Board. So our first plan was to retrieve control of the Board by calling an EGM and, by using the pact, remove Farrell and McGinn – giving us a three-two majority. Any directors co-opted, say the next day, would have to be confirmed at that meeting and the pact would remove them, too. The other plan was to pack the pact with all of the shares of our supporters to ensure that we were not outvoted there. Arrangements were made to get transfers signed through the night.

David phoned me from Heathrow at six-thirty in the morning to discuss the proposed EGM and to confirm that his arrangements were in place with all of the resolutions properly prepared. When Zita looked out of the window, she discovered that we were being doorstepped. The bell went and a woman from the *Evening Times* asked to speak to me. This time, they did not get in. In fact I was determined that they should not get a picture of my leaving the house. So Zita drove off in her car. I jumped over the back garden wall, through the convent garden behind and took over the car from Zita, who walked to my sister's. It cheered me up to outwit them. I knew that it would amuse Chris and David when I got to the Park.

I was first to arrive at eight-thirty, before even the Press – except for the BBC whom Roddy Forsyth had tipped off after speaking to me at home.

I tried to order some food, but that was beyond Celtic's catering. Grant then turned up and I got him to order bacon rolls. I had a chance to talk to him alone in his room. He repeated that the infighting must end and that this was my chance to support McCann. Chris, Kevin and David then arrived. We discussed various options. Then the phone rang for Kevin. He jumped up and never came back. After further discussion with Grant he trumped up an excuse to leave and he never came back, either. Was the embarrassment of their betrayal too much for them?

Poor old Tom. He had been the rebels' foot in the door ever since 1990, the hole in the dyke that they could keep picking away at. How much did he leak to his pals and to the Press over the years? As he plotted and planned for his future that March day, he could not have guessed that before the start of the next season he would have lost his cherished seat on the Board and be stuck with now valueless shares.

The Board met at ten o'clock without McGinn. They proposed the minutes of the previous day's meeting. Under matters arising I read a statement into the minutes to the effect that the meeting was not called with proper notice and no decisions could validly have been taken. I asked why they did what they had done to Chris and David. I reminded them that they knew that Linda was pregnant, despite which they had allowed the letter to be delivered to her home without checking that Chris was there to receive it. Kevin mumbled a bit, but I got no answer. Kevin then moved on to the next item, our resignations. He had to be reminded that we were working on an agreement which might include that, or might not. The meeting was adjourned. I asked Kevin about the rights of my family to get into games. I got the usual equivocation. He left the Boardroom as Grant came back in. So I asked him, with more positive response. As far as he was concerned those kind of things would not change and we would all be welcome in the front door. I told him that I couldn't believe that Kevin would do this to me, as I wouldn't have – and hadn't, for five years – done it to him. But six months later somebody had.

There then followed a series of meetings. Grant came into his room, where the three of us sat all day, to say 'they' wanted to speak to me. I was taken into the players' tea lounge to see Grant, Dominic Keane, Farrell, McGinn and Kevin. I chose my seat with care to face Keane and found myself sitting next to McGinn. Kevin was allowed to speak. He told me that Chris's solicitor had been instructed to do a separate deal for Chris and Adele. He offered me a deal which will 'include your family, Maureen and your mother'. I asked him if it included our mutual cousins, Yvonne and David. Keane muttered, 'Who are they?' Grant was quicker than Kevin to supply the answer. Kevin said that there was only limited money as I was saying, over his words, '. . . and Desmond Barr and Willie Hughes', another mutual cousin and uncle. He replied that more people meant less money for each.

I looked at Grant and repeated that I would not abandon Chris and Adele or anybody else. I told them to offer us the Haughey/Weisfeld deal. Keane was shaking his head, as I pointed out that £3.6m would give them control and treat the shareholders fairly. Keane said that figure included Grant and Kevin, who were staying. 'Even better,' I said, 'it will only cost you £2.6m. Offer that and I will be gone by mid-day, and I will urge the other two to resign.' Keane said no. I told them that I would think about their offer, and that they should think about mine. McGinn and Farrell were desperate to agree that it was reasonable of me to ask this. I left.

I went back and told the other two of the pathetic attempts to split us up. These guys had been so used to betraying each other and us over a period of years that they had forgotten what loyalty was. It never crossed my mind to abandon anybody. Nor did Chris or David waver.

David was then invited to have discussions with them. When he came back, his advice was that we 'cut a deal'. I agreed that this was the sensible decision. But I was willing to fight on. Asking David later why he gave that advice, he said that one look at Chris's face convinced him that he had had enough and that he (David) was not prepared to put him through the extra month's pressure that an EGM would entail. We were also concerned that McCann might withdraw his guarantee, put the Club into receivership and buy it from the bank the next minute. With our experience of the bank we could not expect them to look for the best offer. They just wanted out.

The three of us decided what we would ask for for ourselves, families and friends. I made my decision on price and did not budge from it.

We agreed that David would negotiate on behalf of us all. The negotiations went on back and forward all morning and afternoon. I phoned around the shareholders that I had accepted responsibility for, asking if they wanted to sell. All except Willie Hughes said that they wanted offers.

At about four-thirty it was clear that a deal would be concluded. For the first time, I left Grant's room to see the vultures hovering in the lobby. 'Kevin has handed Celtic over to this mob,' I thought. I went over to shake hands with Dempsey and congratulate him. His hand was cold and sweaty, and he said nothing. I went over to speak to McCann, who was standing with Brendan Mirner and Charles Barnett. The conversation went precisly like this. Me: 'How are you?' Him: 'Oh pretty tired.' Me: 'Look after the Club.' Him: 'I am glad that you are leaving.' I laugh, as he adds: 'And so is everybody else.' Me: 'That's not nice.' Him: 'But it's true.' I laughed, as did everyone else who could hear. Kevin had given Celtic to this man.

This conversation has been reported differently. This version is accurate. I thought it so funny and revealing that I went back to the room, told Chris and David and wrote it down word for word.

I was told I looked tired – thanks to David Bick, David's PR man, phoning me at three in the morning to discuss things! I was angry at looking drawn because I didn't feel under great strain and I didn't want it to appear I was. So I went into the dressing room for a wash. Lou Macari came in as I was drying my hair and we had a wee talk. I told him to get rid of Charlie Nicholas. As we shook hands, my last word to him was that he was to be sure to get two points the next day.

A fish tea in the Walfrid had been laid on for six o'clock. I remembered the meal there before the fateful AGM in 1990. This time, Chris couldn't face eating – but he came in later to join us. I had soup, followed by fried haddock. I was really on a diet for my daughter Teresa's wedding and rarely had three courses anyway. But I knew that the other gang would be watching what we were eating to see if they had put us off our food. So I ordered apple pie

170

and custard. There was none, so I settled for ice cream. Reading Low's book, it was exactly as I thought – he was watching! They were so pedestrian and predictable.

At our table were David Bick, Alastair Dickson and Keith Anderson. I looked at the other table with Kevin, Farrell, Grant, D. Keane, J. Keane, Flannigan, McCann, Jim Dempsey, Brian Dempsey, Low and many hangers-on. I thought: 'This is the table I choose.'

Many of our faithful Celtic staff – including John Maguire – were upset. Mary McAdam and Kay were crying. So was Chris. This irritated me. I told them that it was not a crying matter. I reminded them of the real problems people have with their health or with their families. I also was realistic enough to know that they were sufficiently professional to continue to do their best for the new regime.

The documentation took hours to complete. I could hear the crowd outside chanting 'Michael Kelly's on the dole' before they made their way back to their peripheral houses. McCann greeted them about ten forty-five and they dispersed tooting their horns, uncaring that they had seen the last of the real Celtic. After the lawyers had satisfied themselves with the documentation we all had to gather in the Boardroom for a signing ceremony. I deliberately took a seat away from the table. I had promised that I would never sit around the same boardroom table as Dempsey and his crew and I wanted to keep that promise, literally. Grant made some pathetic comment about the order in which the papers should be signed, ignorant that in Scots law we were all already committed. I told McCann to get on with it, but he didn't respond. Flying in from Canada that morning he had had a very long day (transatlantic commuting of a sort he'll have much less of now that he's got a local base in the shape of *Scotsport*-presenter Jim White's former residence), which possibly accounted for the careless errors in the agreement and the fact that he allowed Weisfeld the chance to gain control of a large percentage of shares.

There followed a Board meeting at eleven o'clock at which Kevin thought that we were going to offer our resignations. He had to be reminded that we had already agreed to resign on the following Friday, if they delivered their side of the deal. This was something that took their advisers by surprise too. But, in my opinion, they weren't in the same league as David's people.

Kevin then thanked us for our services to Celtic in his usual pathetic way and wished us 'and [our] families all the best for the future'. David and Chris wished the Club all the best. I said nothing. Kevin then tried to co-opt McCann and D. Keane, which I was preparing myself to vote against. But David intervened to say that he supposed that they wanted us to withdraw, which we did.

So, there it was, the old guard who had run Celtic down remorselessly over the years were sitting down with the rebels, whose ambition had mortally damaged the Club. And we, who had tried to rectify the damage that had been done over so many years, were gone.

Basically the deal which the three of us concluded with McCann, Dempsey, J. Keane and D. Keane provided that we resign in exchange for their purchasing our shares and those of twenty-one other shareholders, family and supporters – in effect all of those who were not on the other side. We fulfilled our commitment not to leave anyone locked in. Anyone who remained a Celtic shareholder did so by choice.

At the start of the negotiations that Friday, I told David, who was to conduct the discussions, that I wanted £300 per share for all of my immediate family. I never moved from that and was eventually offered that price for myself, Zita, my mother, Maureen and my children. My cousins were offered only £145 per share and non-family supporters were offered only £100. Despite the day-long arguments the other side refused to budge. At the end I told Kevin that I expected him to explain to our cousins, first, why he had turned down a much better offer for them from Weisfeld and, secondly, why he now could not get them a better settlement. He agreed to, but, of course, he never did.

My holding plus those of Zita and the kids realised a gross sum of £208,000, from which has to be deducted the £40,000 I had invested in the shares the previous year. So determined were the twenty-one not to sell to Dempsey and his gang that the vast majority of them went and made their own arrangements with someone else, at much better prices, as it turned out.

It is for Chris, if he wants to, to disclose his agreement. To allow us to get a better deal, David was prepared to lose money on his holding.

But the deceit went on, with Kevin phoning our cousins offering to find a buyer for their shares at a price that had now risen to £300. He told Yvonne that he had been authorised by John Keane to make the offer. David Low then phoned as well, allegedly on behalf of Kevin. My cousin, David Kelly, phoned Kevin to complain and told him his strong objection to being approached by someone who had done his best to discredit the family. What was going on within the group that had taken over was not clear, but it was obvious that the in-fighting had started again within the first week of their seizing control.

The next day, even though it was all over, the Press still could not tell the true story. Dempsey was given credit for the takeover, being hailed as the 'saviour of Celtic' for the simple reason that the Press had portrayed him as such for four years. They were not going to let the fact that it was McCann's intervention that had been crucial spoil the story at that late stage. In fact, it had very little to do with Dempsey at the end. McCann was the one who put the money up, and he gave Dempsey short shrift as far as a seat on the board was concerned. It was then announced that Dempsey was going to the States for a year to eighteen months, (a) to help run the World Cup, (b) for tax reasons, in one of the world's strictest tax regimes, and/or (c) for health reasons, because he had had bronchitis. It is normally sufficient for one reason to be put forward when someone emigrates. But in Dempsey's case, three weren't enough, as he came back two weeks later without arousing any speculation whatsoever.

On 11 March 1994, Chris, David's solicitors and I had gathered in Pannell's offices to complete the deal. The meeting was called for two o'clock, but none of the other side appeared for some considerable time. There was no need for the two sides to meet, but certain details had to be finalised and more documents signed. They were totally disorganised, to the extent that they had forgotten the company seal. They had to send to Celtic Park for Grant to bring it.

The day dragged on and on, with McCann's solicitors hanging about waiting for decisions. Mr Di Ciacca, the partner in the firm he was using, only showed himself at nine o'clock that night. I tried to get some sense out of him as to why everything was taking so long. But he seemed preoccupied. Even the bank drafts, as required by the agreement, were not produced – but we eventually left having tied things up at eleven-fifteen. But not quite tied up. In the agreement their lawyers had so painstakingly drawn up, they forgot to require us to resign as directors of all Celtic's subsidiaries. Six months later, I was still a 'Celtic' director. It could take an EGM to remove me! The 'Bungling Board' could not have done it less efficiently.

All during the week, people crawled out from the undergrowth to declare for the new Board and announce the fact that they had been working away against us in secret. When I heard that McStay claimed to have been set to organise a Spartacus-style players' revolt, I was encouraged because it would have been the first bit of leadership that he had ever shown. The one thing that the Board was united on was that Paul McStay was no captain. We asked both McNeill and Brady to consider giving the job to someone, anyone, else. Here was the player, at last showing some initiative. But Paul is no Wat Tyler (he's no Bobby Murdoch, either, but that's another story) and this latest report turned out to be another disappointment: Paul and the other players were *thinking* about doing something, but never quite got round to it. And, anyway, even if they had submitted transfer requests they weren't going to go anywhere, they said. They were right about that. McStay had put himself in the shop window the previous summer and, as far as anyone on the Board knew, had never even got a tickle. What chance had the rest got, after the season we had had and the wages they were on? But they couldn't even follow through with their master plan. They were talked out of it.

Nicholas was another one that claimed to have opposed the Board, though like McStay he kept it pretty well hidden when I was around. I can understand his bitterness. He was a particularly talented player who, through a series of bad decisions, never fulfilled his early promise. His love of Celtic caused him to leave for Arsenal, where he never made an impression. I saw his resentment against the Board as more a railing at his own wasted career. He also felt that the Club owed him money.

The final act of betrayal was complete. The deceivers were at the door.

174

Chapter Eleven

Pandoemonium, the high capitol
of Satan and his peers . . .

Paradise Lost, 1.756

Right in the middle of the run-up to the first AGM in March 1992, Rangers accused Celtic fans of causing alleged damage to some seats at Ibrox. Trust Mr Murray to exploit a situation. The Rangers secretary, Campbell Ogilvie, wrote to complain: 'We have documented evidence and still photographs which will clearly highlight the culprits although, at this juncture, it would be our preference not to proceed with action through the police authorities.' He warned that future action might include banning Celtic fans. A week later, Chris replied to Ogilvie's letter, challenging over the amount of damage. 'If it is true that you have evidence through video and photographs to identify the culprits,' he wrote, 'then we would strongly advise you to pursue those people via the correct channels, i.e. the police and the courts of law.' Chris pointed out that Rangers fans had damaged Celtic Park.

Although the alleged cause of the dispute was the supposed malicious damage that Murray claimed that Celtic fans had done to the seats in the Broomloan stand, we suspected – wrongly, perhaps – the real reason was so that Rangers could sell season tickets in that part of the ground to their own fans. As long as Celtic fans were to be allowed in, the police would insist on the whole area being segregated. Whereas the same would not apply to the supporters of Aberdeen or Hearts, who couldn't fill the stand anyway.

So every time Celtic went to Ibrox, Rangers made a huge fuss about damage to seats. But when Grant had gone anonymously to the Broomloan stand for a game, he saw no deliberate damage. He did report that, when he got to the ground early, some seats had already been broken (presumably from a previous game), and that some seats were damaged as fans climbed over them to get out of the poorly designed stand.

Officials of both clubs had a wearisome correspondence about the matter, and a series of meetings. Celtic insisted that it would not tolerate hooliganism and urged Rangers to prosecute anyone caught in the act. They refused, as did the police. And, despite our offer of officials from the Club and the supporters association to sift through videos of the crowd, to identify culprits, nothing whatsoever was done in this direction. No one has yet been prosecuted for vandalism in the Broomloan Road stand.

When the first shock of having resigned from the Board had sunk in, my first football thought was to get myself to Ibrox for the Old Firm game for which David Murray had refused to sell Celtic supporters tickets. While still on the Board, I had recommended that the directors should not attend if the fans were to be banned. Now that I was just a supporter, I reckoned that it was my duty to be there!

During and after the game from which Celtic supporters were banned, twenty-six fans were arrested – allowing the *Daily Record* to hail the Rangers fans' behaviour as 'reasonable'. Well, maybe it was in the Press box, but it wasn't from where I was sitting.

A couple of days after I left the Board, I had phoned an old pal and client who I knew had a table in the Thornton Suite. I warned him that my presence might cause comment, but he brushed that aside, pointing out that he paid for his facilities and that there was no prohibition whatsoever on whom he might bring as a guest. And, though he must have had second thoughts as the day came nearer, to his credit he never attempted to back down. So come the day, I was in.

I walked up the marble staircase to the Thornton Suite to be met by an Ibrox official whom I knew. He gave me a warm welcome – then said: 'For God's sake, don't stand up if you score.' One of the Rangers directors came up to me during the meal to shake hands. But I am not very good at it – despite begging David Smith for lessons!

After lunch I was standing alone waiting until the last possible moment to go up to my seat, when first one guy then another sidled up to me to say, 'It's OK. You're not alone.' I sat down in an atmosphere more hateful than usual, whipped up as it was by supporters songs that I had not previously heard over the PA at old firm games. The Rangers fan sitting near me turned around and said: 'What are you doing here?' Then he added, 'I was in Leeds when Rangers supporters were banned. I understand.'

When Gough fouled young Donnelly just outside the box, I claimed the free kick. The same guy leaned across and said, again jokingly, 'Look, you're not even supposed to be here, never mind commenting.' 'Yeah, it was a terrible decision,' I said. 'Just don't jump up if it goes in,' he said. 'Don't worry,' I replied. 'I'll just hug you.'

Collins did score, in virtually total silence. I sat without moving a muscle. But around me Rangers fans stood up to see if anyone was cheering. Their witch-hunt identified three fans whom they took to be supporting Celtic. Another client of mine was sitting behind these three and said that, without standing up, one of them made the most suppressed signs of pleasure. But it was enough – at the behest of the mob, all three were escorted out. I later found out that the culprit was a Motherwell supporter whose team still had a chance of winning the League, and his two pals were Rangers supporters.

The next ten minutes were extremely threatening. I kept thinking: 'This is the kind of thing that leads to Auschwitz.' Over in the Rangers-end stand, I could see more alleged Celtic fans being removed by stewards and police. A shower of coins descended on them as they went.

When I went downstairs at half-time, one of the lounge stewards asked me if I was happy with the score. 'I'm not allowed to be happy,' I replied. He told me that the three who had been escorted from the stand had asked if they could return to the lounge to await their hosts. The request had been refused and they had been thrown out of the stadium.

I had promised David that I would phone him from Ibrox. As I was stuffing money into the lounge coin-box, a couple of Rangers supporters went past. 'Is that you phoning Parkhead for the half-time score?' asked one. 'No, I'm phoning for a taxi,' I joked. 'Fucking get one,' said his pal. Rangers require the highest standard of behaviour in the Thornton Suite. Everyone must wear a jacket and tie.

When Rangers equalised in the second half, a hooligan sitting outwith the businessmen's section about six rows in front of me and about twenty-five seats in, ran from his seat up the passage way to stand at my row, gesturing obscenely and shouting abuse. The stewards looked on helplessly.

The only other memory I have of that game is the appalling state of the pitch. The state of the playing surface at Ibrox had been so bad the previous season that Rangers had spent £300,000 on lowering the pitch and re-turfing it. Despite this expenditure, that day it looked like a ploughed field. I thought of the criticism the 'Bungling Board' would have been subjected to if the same had happened to Celtic Park. But, of course, not a word. I mentioned this to a reporter on the night of the game. 'Well,' he said, 'Stuart McCall told the Press after the game that even A.C. Milan couldn't play on a pitch like that, so maybe you'll see something tomorrow.' Not a chance.

On the way home from the game, the Rangers supporter who had offered me a lift reminded me of the story of Johnny Little, the 1950s Rangers full-back to whom Scot Symon had given the choice: 'Your Catholic girlfriend or Rangers.' So little seemed to have changed. And so few people have really tried to change it.

This brought me back to much more fundamental issues: the nasty side of human nature. What I witnessed at Ibrox was not unique to Rangers supporters. It was merely a minor manifestation of the worldwide phenomenon of intolerance and discrimination. But I did not need to go beyond the East End of Glasgow for an example. Over the past four years, I have seen exactly the same kind of venom from Celtic supporters directed at me. Aimed at a rival group, it is seen as amusing and condoned. Being on the receiving end makes you appreciate that it is the very stuff of fascism. I had begun to see how obscene it must look through outsiders' eyes. For years I had wanted to believe that the Celtic support was different. I could see now how farcical that notion would appear to the Rangers directors who had sat at Celtic Park the previous New Year's Day, afraid for life and limb. They could have written an account of that day which exactly mirrored my experience at Ibrox.

I sat down in the house trying to sort out my feelings about Celtic. I could not move from the conclusion that the dirty campaign of 1990-94 had destroyed the Celtic ethic. While there are broader social reasons why the attitude and outlook of Celtic supporters have changed from that of the previous generation, there is no doubt that the campaign against the

Board pushed the Club in the direction of the worst element of the support. It was the bad driving out the good. The decent supporters were disgusted by the behaviour that the propaganda triggered off among a large minority of their fellow fans. It will be very difficult to persuade those good people to return, with the unpleasantness so fresh in their minds. And many of them never will. In that fundamental sense, the campaign was against the interests of the Club. In addition, the people who were prepared to resort to the tactics that were employed against us are not able to carry on the Celtic tradition. They do not begin to understand what it means. Some fans still do, and it is within them that the spark still flickers. The feeling for what Celtic is really about surely still exists among thousands of real Celtic supporters – supporters who understand the broader motives of the Club's founders, and who care for the traditions that developed from those aspirations throughout a century of struggle and achievement. Such supporters abhorred the savage and despicable tactics directed against the Club in a blatant attempt by a small group of people to seize control. These supporters must, like me, feel that the Club has lost its unique personality.

But everything is not lost. Nothing can erase the part that the Club played in the fight against poverty and discrimination and for social justice. Perhaps what Celtic offered one hundred years ago is not so badly needed now, since the immigrant community from which it sprang is so well integrated. But the Celtic traditions and values have a broader application, and they may be needed here again. True Celtic supporters will not allow their children to forget.

The real purpose and achievements of Celtic Football Club will continue to inspire as long as folk history is cherished and recounted – and the struggle written of in this book is part of that history.

But for now and for the foreseeable future, Celitic is just another football team. It is now a business. So its success must be judged solely in terms of how many trophies it wins and how much money it makes.

The fascination for me over the next few years will be to see how well McCann is able to run the Club, after being so critical of our performance. My judgment is that he will not succeed in meeting the heightened expectations of the fans which his propaganda generated. On the field, he must achieve immediate success – otherwise the intolerance among the fans which the rebels have bred will quickly be turned on him. They are now on a shorter fuse.

But if winning trophies is going to be difficult, the long-term business success is going to be even harder to produce. The impression I got from him all along, and the main reason that I thought an accommodation with him unlikely, was that he appears not to understand the Scottish and European football environments as they now exist. And he over-estimates the commercial value of the Celtic brand name. In short, I think that he will lose his money. I think it is highly unlikely that he will be able to sell out to the fans in five years' time, if that is still his plan. In fact, I'm sure that the fans won't be daft enough to take up more than a small fraction of the currently proposed issue of voteless preference shares. Certainly, three months after the takeover, for the second time in his relationship with McCann, Dempsey had discovered a reason not to put money up.

McCann's dilemma is captured in the fact that so long after his taking over, no significant sums of money have been spent on new players, despite four years of promises that a change in control would bring an immediate injection of money for transfers. On the other hand, after decades of resistance begun by my uncle, the board has meekly agreed to numbers despoiling the hoops (as if everyone didn't know who the Celtic players were). And the decision has been taken to move out of Celtic Park to allow it to be re-built as a 60,000 all-seater stadium. No time scale is given, which may tell the story, because having studied the physical and financial challenges involved in this, I am prepared to state categorically that it will never be finished.

The finances of football are complex and I wonder if McCann fully understands them even yet. It is sensible, in fact given Celtic's aspirations, essential to make the assumption that revenues from games alone will not produce the necessary income. In my view, this must be supplemented either by producing a team capable of the level of performance that leads to bigger crowds, extra games and additional TV receipts, or by use of the stadium facilities for non-football purposes. In addition, modern facilities generate revenue from increased sponsorship and better revenue per head of spectator. Traditionally, football grounds do not generate other revenues. That is the difference that Cambuslang would have made, but something that will be absent at the revamped Celtic Park.

Not that McCann does not recognise the importance of facilities. He does. And he is also entitled to carp that Celtic should have tackled the stadium problem many years ago. But his problem is funding the re-building of the stadium option at the same time as seeking success on the park.

His whole emphasis is, as it always was, on marketing. His assumption is, I believe, wrong. The demand for Celtic products, whether it be games, pies or strips, is not elastic in terms of price or promotion and will not readily respond, apart from an initial burst of enthusiasm, however slick the sell. Revenues respond overwhelming to one thing – the success of the team. In the short-run that must be seen to be linked to buying better players. My doubt is that there is sufficient money available to do that given the commitment to massive investment in the stadium.

Certainly, now that Celtic Park has been demolished we are past the point of no return. What happens now if the money isn't there?

The other fundamental point is to have clear what the overriding objective of the investment and management is. There is a difference between treating football as a business and running a football club in a business-like way, and I am not sure McCann appreciates that.

As I was ruminating, my son David came into the room. We began discussing that afternoon's Rangers game and the silence instilled by John Collins' free-kick. I forgot all about the trauma and felt only the warm glow that comes with an excellent performance and a moral victory.

'Thank God,' I thought. 'I'm still a Celtic supporter.'